Style
Forever

HOW TO LOOK FABULOUS AT EVERY AGE

Style Forever

HOW TO LOOK FABULOUS AT EVERY AGE

ALYSON WALSH

ILLUSTRATED BY LEO GREENFIELD

CONTENTS

INTRODUCTION

SAY HELLO TO *GENERATION FAB* (FIFTY AND BEYOND)

Age is all the rage. And it's about bloody time. I've never really understood why women beyond their childbearing years are cast aside like last season's It-bag. I'm 51 and I'm not interested in airbrushed images of teenage models and age-defying celebrities. I'm not going to mess with my face, I'd rather look old than odd. And I'm not alone. There's a whole generation of women who are independent, intelligent and happy just the way they are. Women who don't buy into the anti-ageing, younger is better model and the pressure to look a certain way. Who refuse to be patronised by unrealistic images and prefer to see women they can relate to. Models who are ageing naturally (or at least appear to be), who look good and look like themselves, and that doesn't equate with looking younger. Meet *Generation FAB* (Fifty And Beyond).

Since the 1960s, fashion has been fixated by youth but fortunately it really does feel like the times they are a-changing. We're finally seeing more gorgeous grown-up women in advertisements, online and in the media. Hallelujah. The over-50s are having a bit of a fashion moment. Pass the Menoforce, I think I'm having a hot flush.

Fashion loves a fad, and having worked in the industry for decades, I'm not going to get carried away when a scattering of brands use older models; but I do think that this is a proper shift in attitudes. *Harper's Bazaar* editor Justine Picardie concurs, 'This is not just a passing trend; brands have done detailed research, and realised that their key consumers are women over the age of 40 – in many cases over the age of 50 – who are affluent, financially independent, sophisticated, and who don't want to be patronised with inappropriate advertising campaigns.'

As a fashion editor, I've spent the majority of my career championing *Generation FAB*. After seven years at *Good Housekeeping* magazine (hardly a temple of high fashion, I know, but it's not all recipes and stain removal), I got an itch to go freelance. Aged 40, I found myself working as a part-time university lecturer and regular contributor to a couple of popular websites. As the only academic in the Journalism Department with any relevant experience, I became the online expert, by default. I didn't even know what blogging was at that juncture but I made it my duty to find out. I set up my blog, *That's Not My Age*, during one of my summer holidays, partly to stay one step ahead of the students and partly because I felt that there was a gap in the blogosphere for someone to talk about grown-up fashion and style in a friendly, intelligent, non-patronising way. And not long after I'd figured out how not to post all my content in the sidebar, my social media addiction kicked in. Networking with lots of engaging women of a similar age was brilliant. I was hooked.

FABsters live longer and we stay fit, look after ourselves and care about our appearance. Aging isn't what it used to be. Self-image is not what it used to be. When you've rocked out to The Rolling Stones or pogo-ed to the Sex Pistols, rebelling against stringent fashion rules and wearing what you please is all part of the norm. Women with a lifelong interest in fashion and popular culture don't just switch off the minute the body clock strikes 40. 'These are the same women who are reading *Harper's Bazaar*,' says Justine Picardie, 'And they're a tremendously powerful demographic that can no longer be ignored by ad agencies. Many of them define themselves as being feminist, as well as being interested in fashion; the two are not mutually exclusive. And they are therefore far more likely to identify with advertising campaigns and editorial that features strong, grown-up women. All in all, it's a hugely positive development.'

'Young. Old. Just words.'
– George Burns

Social networking has played a major role in this development; blogging has provided a show-and-tell platform and a support network that just wasn't available within traditional media. Easily accessible information and 24-hour shopping are just a swipe of a smartphone away. Now it's possible to buy what you like, when you like, and then show it to the world. There's a power that comes from this increased visibility of older women online – this is what we look like, this is what we wear; get over it. Though as we've seen on Twitter, this can involve having to fight back against the forces of reaction. 'Clothes are really empowering, fashion is empowering,' points out Matches Fashion co-founder Ruth Chapman, 'I don't think we should be restricted, the possibilities are endless. There is something really attractive about a woman who is confident about her age and style.'

This new mood puts me in mind of the late Diana Vreeland. The legendary fashion editor celebrated diversity by encouraging women to be proud of their unconventionality, turning Barbara Streisand's 'Nefertiti nose' and Lauren Hutton's gappy smile into wonderful attributes in American *Vogue* in the 1960s. Using diverse models to break the mould sent out an important message at the time, and this creative vision, together with Vreeland's eloquent pronouncements, turned her into one of the most influential women of twentieth-century fashion. And I can almost feel this attitude and pizzazz fizzing around today. The artist Sue Kreitzman calls it the Old Lady Revolution. *Generation FAB* is pushing traditional media to become more inclusive, to stop dismissing women as past their sell-by date. Old is the new (far more interesting) young.

That's Not My Age allowed me to start a conversation about grown-up style. To share advice and ideas, meet FABulous women and, most of all, have a laugh. I did sometimes wonder if I was also having a midlife crisis online, but gone are the wobbly 'is-this-it' days of my mid-40s. I am my age and I'm happy with that. I strongly believe that you don't have to have youth to have style. That it's not about age, it's about mindset. This book continues the conversation with some of my favourite style heroines. These are role models, industry experts and women of substance who inspire me with their attitude and achievements. I hope it will help you remain stylish forever.

'I do think the infantalisation of our generation is one of the human issues of our time. People wanting to be 35 when they're 50 makes me think: why? Why don't you be 50 and be good at that?'

– Emma Thompson

YOU'RE NEVER TOO OLD FOR

1

SILK PYJAMAS

2

LEOPARD-PRINT

3

KOOKY SUNGLASSES

4

THE LATEST 'IT' TRAINERS

5

A NEW HOBBY/FRIEND/ LIPSTICK

6

DENIM
(see Iris Apfel on page 32)

7

PILATES

8

VINTAGE
Even if it's not really vintage, just something you've had for a very long time.

9

CHANDELIER EARRINGS

10

ROCK AND ROLL
(and parties, usually of the Big-0 variety).

ELEMENTS OF STYLE

Accepting who you are and being comfortable in your own skin, even if it is a bit saggy, comes with grown-up territory. It's over a decade ago now, but I spent most of my 39th year feeling sorry for myself. Poor me. Single, no kids and no sign of the *Elle Decoration*-ready house I'd imagined: all space, light and perfect pale wood flooring. But I was living the dream. As a fashion editor on a glossy magazine, day-to-day business involved going on fashion shoots to exotic locations – some of them abroad – being schmoozed by PRs proffering cheap champagne, meeting fabulous women like Nigella Lawson and Yasmin Le Bon and performing reader makeovers. Every month. Without fail. You know, the kind of thing that made Trinny & Susannah famous but without the bullying, and, if I say so myself, with much better styling. After years of tirelessly making over loyal readers,

friends and family members (not mine, mostly my assistant's Mum who got a taste for the high life), when it comes to dressing well, I know all the tricks. What works and what doesn't – and that when people don't like having their photograph taken, you give them alcohol. As Trinny & Susannah's post-makeover victims prove, a decent hairstyle and well-applied make-up go a long way. Add the right clothes – and I don't mean the right clothes in a bossy boots, fashion dictator sense, I mean the right clothes for you – and I believe that, regardless of the barriers of money, age and social class, every woman can look gorgeous.

As every FABster knows, paying attention to the cut and curve of your clothes and the details, pays off in the long run. I've listed what I know on the following pages (and it's not all fashion bollocks).

IT'S ALL ABOUT THE FIT

There are a few fashion items that are worth spending money on: a decent jacket, good shoes and proper underwear. I'm not going to go on about bras here – if you want my advice, buy decent French lingerie and replace it on a regular basis. (Hark at me I sound like Diana Vreeland). Anyhow. When I was a fashion student, I did a six-month work placement at a men's suit factory in Bradford. Hardly Yves Saint Laurent Le Smoking territory, I know, but this is where I learnt some of the tricks of the tailoring trade and discovered the numerous processes that go into making an off-the-peg jacket. I also learnt that drinking cider with the warehouse boys is never a good way to start the day, you're always half asleep by 4 o'clock.

With tailoring you definitely get what you pay for. A cheap jacket is always going to look like a cheap jacket – and sometimes that's fine – but mostly it's worth spending a bit more on a superior fabric and fit. Kathryn Sargent is known as the only female tailor on Savile Row; having trained at Gieves & Hawkes for 15 years, she recently moved just around the corner to set up her own bespoke business.

Having learnt her trade working on menswear, Kathryn initially started making garments for herself, in order to look smarter when meeting clients. Experimenting with patterns, she would change the shape and style of various jackets and pretty soon her male customers started introducing her to their wives and female colleagues: CEOs, bankers and women who work in the legal profession. All of whom appreciate the heritage of Savile Row tailoring and the allure of beautiful British fabrics. At a meeting in Kathryn's London showroom, she talks me through her craft and explains how shaping and detail can help change the form of a jacket. Pulling items from a rail to illustrate the subtle differences in cut and construction. It's a million miles from the menswear factory in Bradford, and we're on coffee not cider, but the basic principles are the same.

To someone who embraces Casual Glamour, the kick-ass jacket is a vital carapace thrown on over jeans and a T-shirt for business meetings, or to help avoid the ghastly lecturer-dressed-as-student vibe. Not forgetting that when everything starts to slip southwards, a spot of decent tailoring can help to restore a little structure and conceal the dreaded middle-age spread.

I can't afford bespoke but I do know that whatever the price tag, fit across the shoulders is paramount and should be the first consideration. It's also good to know a decent tailor who can alter off-the-peg purchases. Sleeve length is a personal choice – some people like longer to the base of the thumb (good for rolling up), others a shorter length allowing a shirt cuff to peep out. Jacket length is influenced by the wearer's body shape; the boyfriend-style blazer is an excellent cover-up for a range of different silhouettes, just opt for a semi-fitted style if you're curvy or have big boobs. While the cropped, collarless 50s number is perfect for petite frames and pear shapes.

'It depends where things lie,' adds Kathryn, 'I'm not a perfect size eight so I like to cover my seat. It depends what you want to achieve, to enhance the curves or look androgynous.'

PROPORTION, PROPORTION, PROPORTION

The late Professor Louise Wilson was head of the MA course at Central Saint Martins college, London, and as well as being a formidable tutor to some of the great British designers like Alexander McQueen, Roksanda Ilincic and Christopher Kane, she was an expert when it came to proportion. She was a big woman in all senses of the word, and I'm sure Louise wouldn't have minded me saying that. We worked together for a T-shirt company when I first moved to London and I can still remember her booming voice on the other end of the phone demanding cake be delivered down to the design floor whenever it was a colleague's birthday. Louise was a proper fashion maven and always dressed all in black. There is a gorgeous photo where she's receiving an OBE, with husband Timmy. Louise is wearing an embroidered, shot silk, thigh-length kimono jacket, a pair of cropped trousers and ankle boots. She looked divine.

Now, apologies if I'm stating the bleeding obvious here – I know, the last thing you need is some daft fashion editor telling you what to do – but there is a rather basic style equation. Generally speaking, when it comes to proportion and balance, a looser top looks better

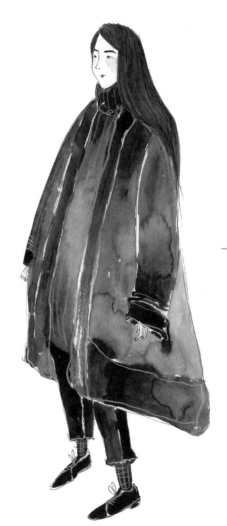

over slim pants or a pencil skirt and a looser bottom half (wide-leg trousers or A-line skirt) looks neater with a more streamlined top. After all, no one wants to look like a Stop Making Sense-era David Byrne. Explaining his oversized beige suit at the time, the art-rocker revealed, 'I wanted my head to look smaller and the easiest way was to make my body bigger.' Enough said.

HOW TO DO BOHO WITHOUT LOOKING LIKE A HOBO (AND AM I TOO OLD FOR VINTAGE?)

I did live in a squat once, dress in shabby second-hand clothes and cut my own hair, but I wouldn't call that bohemian. I'd call that being a student. And what is boho, anyway? The posho Mitford sisters gadding about the countryside in ballgowns and wellington boots? Patti Smith 'machete-ing her way out of the folk era' with a DIY Keith Richards haircut? Keith Richards with a Keith Richards haircut and carry-on bag of pharmaceuticals, being stopped at every airport in the 1970s? Artists, writers and musicians? Over the centuries the term 'bohemian' has largely been used to refer to creative outsiders who live and dress to please themselves. People who travelled the globe pre-budget airlines and could throw an unconventional look together based on items acquired en route such as: appliquéd smocks, embroidered silks and fringed paisley scarves. Originally applied to the 19th century Roma gypsies of central Europe, bohemian was a

derogatory label, and has come full circle in fashion today. Every summer, Patrick Lichfield's late 1960s photo of socialite Talitha Getty (on a rooftop in Marrakech) does the rounds, alongside a pile of cheap embroidered kaftans and tops. Though I loathe this commodification, I'm not a stranger to a handy beach cover-up.

The 1970s had everything: hippies, punks, disco, new wave. I just wish I'd been a bit older so I could've enjoyed it more. Throughout the decade, mainstream fashion was rejected for second-hand clothes from the 30s and 40s, military garb and DIY style. Designers like Ossie Clarke and Celia Birtwell in London and Yves Saint Laurent in Paris/ Marrakech tuned into these early eras for inspiration. Vivienne Westwood and Malcolm MacLaren rehashed the 1950s Teddy Boy look before letting rip with sex, sleaze and safety pins.

The 1970s is often referred to as the decade that style forgot, but I'm with Diana Vreeland on the prospect of too much good taste: 'A little bad taste is like a nice splash of paprika. We all need a splash of bad taste, it's hearty, it's healthy, it's physical. I think we could use more of it. No taste is what I'm against.'

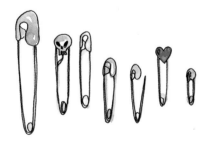

There's a fashion myth that once you get to a certain vintage, you can no longer wear vintage – that's rubbish. Everyone can wear second-hand stuff, just as long as it doesn't smell. And following this edict would rule out those much-loved items that are so old they're practically vintage anyway. Those clothes and accessories accumulated over the years with sentimental value or that better-keep-hold-of-it-just-in-case feel, not to mention any recent charity shop finds. Though good luck with those, my local charity shops are all full of unwanted Primark T-shirts and *Top Gear* boxsets. No. There are many older women who wear vintage clothes beautifully: Catherine Baba the avant-garde Paris-based stylist, Virginia Bates the former boutique owner, actress and co-author of the style book *Jazz Age Fashion: Dressed to Kill*, always looks stunning in an array of embellished, ankle-length frocks, opera coats and kick-ass jackets. The trademark brightly coloured trilby perched atop her bleached-blonde bob and a stack of beaded necklaces helps to frame a beautiful, impeccably made-up face. I'd say New Yorker Iris Apfel is a true bohemian too. Wearing her fashion history on her sleeve, the nonagenarian's flamboyant, more-is-more approach practically tells her life story – as well as revealing a strong sense of style and an extremely good eye. As Harold Koda, curator of the Costume Institute at the Metropolitan Museum said, 'To dress this way, there has to be an educated visual sense.' Apfel and her husband Karl ran their own interior design business, Old

World Weavers, providing furnishings and curtains for the White House through nine successive presidencies. Wearing big bold glasses the size of petri dishes, with baubles and bangles piled on, she was the subject of a Met Museum exhibition, coffee table book (*A Rare Bird of Fashion* by photographer Eric Boman) and documentary by *Grey Gardens'* filmmaker Albert Maysles. The self-proclaimed Geriatric Starlet has been collecting clothes and jewellery since she was 11 and quips, 'I like old things, vintage, things that look old – makes me look better.'

Of course, there are no rules on how to 'do' bohemian. Though I'd recommend keeping the silhouette simple by choosing clean lines over ruffles, frills and frou-frou. A flat canvas creates a more elegant look: Iris Apfel often starts with a tunic over trousers, Virginia Bates with a slinky floor-length gown, finished off with a mountain of fabulous jewellery and a show-stopping coat. Perfect.

THE FABULOUS GUIDE TO COLOUR

'I live, breathe and dream about colour,' the artist Sue Kreitzman tells me when I visit her London home. The entire house is like one great big art installation; a living museum full of kitsch and creative clutter. Every single wall is painted red and decorated with artwork and collages, every surface covered with Sue's own sculptures, made from found objects, mannequins and doll's heads. It's a treasure trove of the bizarre – and

it's brilliant. 'The older I get, the more technicolour my world becomes,' she tells me as we settle into two scarlet armchairs. 'I've roamed the world looking for saturation and intensity.' She goes on to advise me that I should be wearing my black overalls with brighter accessories, 'Black is great but you need to splash it with colour. I wish people would be bolder.' This isn't the first time Sue and I have met; that was at a London College of Fashion conference on fashion, ageing and culture where Ari Seth Cohen and I gave a talk about our blogs and the impact online culture has had on the visibility of older women. She and Ari have been friends since 2009, when he took her photograph on the street outside New York's New Museum. The Fabulous Fashionista gave me a makeover. Decked out in one of her beautiful Lauren Shanley coats, with armfuls of rubbery bangles and a necklace made from decorative plastic combs, I felt like a rock star. Sue is a fantastic, inspirational woman and I was delighted to be turned into a work of art.

As someone who usually spends her life in neutrals, I felt surprisingly comfortable at saturation point. Khaki, denim and shades of blue and grey form my regular colour palette – though I'll occasionally break out the fancy pants or fluorescent-pink trainers (both of which are easy to avoid in the mirror). Christian Dior once advised, 'Two colours in any outfit are quite enough.' and I've always been inclined to agree. Subtle tones are easy to match, easy to wear and can, when required, provide the perfect, attention-swerving camouflage.

'Don't wear beige, it might kill you,' is Sue's motto. And while I completely understand where she's coming from – I've seen people who have taken that dreary greige route and their clothes, hair and complexion all end up looking the same shade. But I do love the warmer tones of camel, tobacco and donkey brown, and worn the right way (I'm thinking cashmere), these can look incredibly elegant. And anyway what about the Burberry trench, surely that's a design classic? 'I say it's beige and I say the hell with it!' exclaims FABulous Sue. 'It makes me feel old and it makes me feel ill. I have a phobia. It's a visceral thing. Coffee, latte, whatever they call it – I say it's beige and I say stay away from it.'

HOW TO WEAR BEIGE WITHOUT IT KILLING YOU:

1. Avoid yellowy beige, choose warmer shades and call it camel. Now, doesn't that feel better?

2. Team camel with a strong colour: red, black or leopard print, or all of the above, in winter. Turquoise and white in summer, and Bob's your uncle.

Stick to natural fibres like cashmere, wool, silk, and linen. Avoid nasty man-made fabrics – they will make you want to kill yourself.

AND HOW TO WEAR COLOUR
WITHOUT LOOKING LIKE A
CRAZY LADY:

1. Make like a Mondrian painting and wear blocks of colour. Monochrome plus a primary colour creates a powerful visual effect. Orange, turquoise and emerald green also look stunning with black and white. Sue Kreitzman is right about pepping up an all-black outfit, though I'd go easy on the plastic accessories.

2. Walk into Cos and see how wonderful a blast of neon colour looks against a navy or grey backdrop.

3. Stick to one colour head to toe.

4. Wishy washy pastel hues have no place in a grown-up woman's wardrobe. Too insipid. Too girlie. Too mother-of-the-bride. Faded denim is the nearest to a sugar-coated shade allowed. Don't wear pastels they might not kill you but they will make you look 20 years older.

5. Mix it up – it is possible to go mental and look wonderful.

THE ART OF LAYERING

Layering is basically wearing one thing on top of another and we do it all the time. Mostly to keep warm, but also to subtly change the body's proportions. Eileen Fisher recommends getting the underpinnings right. By underpinnings,

the chic American designer and High Priestess of Layering means a long jersey tank. This is placed underneath a shorter knitted top and worn over straight leg trousers or a knee-length/maxi skirt. Said underpinning slinks over the hips providing coverage without adding unnecessary bulk. My good friend, the fashion writer and academic, Brenda Polan concurs, 'I always recommend a long-sleeved fine-knit T-shirt because you can put anything over it – like a cardigan or gilet – and take the layers off again during a hot flush. White or black T-shirts are a good starting point, they coordinate with everything and virtually disappear.'

But layers can quite easily flip from elegant and swish to frumpy and sloppy. And no one wants to look frumpy and sloppy. Even though the aim is always to look effortless, outfits need to be properly thought out and coordinated, not just slung together. Choose colours that work together like navy and charcoal; if that sounds a bit sensible then add a colourful underpinning and some bling-tastic jewellery. With layers, either a necklace that sits at the base of the neck or a longer Chatelaine style is best. Other factors to consider include fabric quality and colour consistency. Good-quality, well-cut natural fabrics with a little Lycra tend to drape better and last longer than the cheaper alternatives. Head-to-toe matching colour creates a flattering column shape. For further proof see Dame Judi Dench at the Skyfall premiere (and I still can't believe they killed her off). Get it right and look sassy and modern. Get it wrong and look like a bag lady.

THE FINAL FLOURISH: ACCESSORIES AND OTHER SUCH FRIPPERIES

THE FACE-FLATTERING, OUTFIT-ENHANCING SCARF

I've noticed that, as I get older, like a decent cup of overpriced, artisan coffee, scarves are becoming an important part of everyday life. Anyone can wear a scarf, but having the panache to carry one off is a completely different matter. Of course I have a best-dressed list: managing director of the International Monetary Fund Christine Lagarde shows that excellent scarf action and power dressing aren't mutually exclusive, Channel 4 News's international editor Lindsey Hilsum uses the versatile accessory to add personality to a functional outfit, while Dame Judi Dench often wears one on the red carpet – though I never feel entirely comfortable with that scarf over the shoulder look. I used to work with a powerful woman who always had a pashmina draped over one of her enormous shoulder pads, and I spent far too much time on the lookout for spontaneous scarf slippage. Nevertheless, all of these women appreciate that there's more to the fine art of accessorising than merely keeping the neck (and shoulder) warm.

Whether you wear one loose, looped or knotted, nonchalance is key. 'To me, scarves look best when worn relaxed and easy,' advises Ruby Chadwick, accessories and jewellery buyer for Liberty. 'They are best when adapted to your personal style and lifestyle, worn loosely over a jacket or shirt to step it up.' In my mind, the perfect scarf has to be lightweight and made of natural fibres, such as silk, cotton or cashmere.

Now is not the right time (of life) to be encasing your neck in Aran wool. And although I adore simplicity, when it comes to neckwear, I'm not averse to bold colour, patterns, tassles and trims. They make for brilliant, outfit-enhancing scarf action, particularly when juxtaposed with a smart tailored jacket or worn to liven up denim or khaki for a spot of Hilsum-style casual glamour.

Mary Berry once showed me how she tied her scarf; it was a complicated manoeuvre and I had to ask her to repeat it several times. By the fourth attempt, she was getting quite exasperated, but fortunately her assistant videoed the whole proceeding and having watched the clip a thousand times I can now confirm that this is how you tie the Mary Berry Knot. See the instructions opposite.

Though I'm not quite at the Nora Ephron stage just yet, I do thoroughly understand the benefits of a beautiful scarf. As Mary Berry points out, they 'cover a scraggy neck'. Just don't drape over one shoulder.

'I'm just trying to change the world, one sequin at a time.'

– Lady Gaga

MARY BERRY'S SCARF KNOT
(BEST DONE WITH A LONGISH SCARF)

1

Loop the scarf around your neck once and make sure that it hangs down evenly on both sides.

2

Reach the right hand through the loop (as if it were a sling) and grab the left hand side of the scarf.

3

Partially pull the left-hand side through the loop to create another loop and hold it there.

4

Pull the right-hand side of the scarf through the left-hand loop.

5

Pull both ends to even up.

BRING ON THE BLING

'Jewellery is all about expressing yourself and the desire to stand out doesn't just disappear as you get older,' points out Harriet Vine of Tatty Devine who, along with design partner Rosie Wolfenden, has been making and designing jewellery since 1999. 'I think personal style constantly evolves and develops. Jewellery is a really easy and fun way to communicate your character and personality, whether you're 20-years-old or 80.' And she's right. Bringing on the bling is an excellent way to liven up an everyday outfit and show a little personality – not forgetting that a sparkly necklace reflects the light back up onto the face, a bit like

having your own portable Instagram filter. Tatty Devine's take is witty and playful and Perspex-oriented, and Harriet champions an older and bolder attitude, 'I'm a really big fan of Ari Seth Cohen's blog *Advanced Style* and constantly inspired by the colourful, vibrant ladies featured.' When it comes to stand-out accessories, Bec Astley Clarke, founder of online luxury jewellery store Astley Clarke agrees, 'Our customers love colour; blue gemstones are popular, as are Morganite (a peachy-pink stone) and grey aquamarine. People want something unusual.' The luxury brand is very much about taking a modern approach to collectable jewellery. 'Over 35, women stop wearing costume and start to take their jewellery box more seriously. I'm 41 and I don't really want to wear it. Precious jewellery is so incredibly special. I firmly believe that if you've made the investment, then you should wear it every day.'

As a fan of a more casual kind of glamour myself, I know that with adornment, a little goes a long way. Being common as muck, I'm definitely at the costume end of the jewellery spectrum, and always like to pair the rough with the smooth. It must be something to do with growing up in a rundown seaside town, but I'll wear a favourite grey sweatshirt with a diamante party necklace, or denim shirt with faux Liz Taylor earrings. OK, so I'm not the first to use eye-catching accessories to help crank up the glamour factor; Coco Chanel famously wore costume jewellery with sporty separates for a relaxed daytime look – and, today – J. Crew's Jenna Lyons has got that high-low look down to a tee. Bec Astley Clarke has a more elegant take

on this phenomenon: 'Personally, I like a bit of juxtaposition between jewellery and clothes. I'm always in jeans – I don't want to look uber-fashionable, I want to look sophisticated. So I'll wear them with a designer silk blouse and the simple decorative elements come with nice shoes, handbags and fine jewellery.' When it comes to fashion, there's definitely an age where buying this season's latest must-have becomes of little interest and longevity becomes key and Bec believes that the same applies to jewellery, 'I do think that women become more interested in fine jewellery as they get older.' She adds, 'Less interested in throwaway fashion. Precious jewellery is something they can hold onto, it has an inherent value that doesn't go away, so they don't feel guilty about buying it and can pass it down. It becomes an heirloom: the silk scarf disintegrates, the shoes don't fit, but the jewellery keeps.'

Basically, it's all a matter of taste, personality and knowing what goes with what. I love a small sprinkling of glitz, so most days you'll find me wearing spangly earrings and an armful of bracelets, yet like Joni Mitchell I'm also happy to 'put on some silver'. There's a set of bangles that have adorned my wrist for over a decade – I never take them off, even for airport security – and a pair of hoop earrings that I turn to to give my lobes a rest from the chandelier styles. Whether it's simple or statement, costume or precious, jewellery is the perfect complement to a pared-down outfit and an easy way to express creativity. I know this from my fashion editor days when styling fashion shoots; a string of gobstopper beads and a stack of bangles

or rings would bring an outfit to life. The devil, as they say, is always in the detail. And size doesn't matter. 'You don't always have to go big,' advises Harriet, 'I often layer smaller fine necklaces for impact. I love wearing my Tatty Devine sterling silver Chip Fork Necklace with family heirlooms and vintage pieces I've picked up at car boot fairs.' Now, to me, that sounds like the ideal arrangement. You can take the girl out of Blackpool...

THE CHIC WAY TO WEAR TRAINERS

My first pair of trainers came from The Catalogue. Remember the days before the internet when clothes were either hand-me-downs or mail order? Forms were neatly filled in and sent off, goods delivered weeks later, when you'd forgotten what you'd ordered. Which was just as well

because half the time Littlewoods didn't have it in stock and would send something else instead, something inferior. We were far too polite to query this system – I don't think we ever sent anything back. And so I was stuck with a pair of black leather Gola Harriers instead of a pair of Adidas SL 72s. Wilfully dragging my feet along the ground as I cycled around the local park, I'd worn my first pair of trainers out before my mum had even completed the never-ending weekly payments.

As a sporty kid, I spent my life kicking around in trainers and I'm still a fan of this laid-back look. To me, a pair of trainers teamed with a tailored jacket and slim or slouchy pants are an essential part of dressed down daywear (see pages 30–31). Think Coco Chanel wafting along the French Riviera in wide leg trousers, Mick Jagger's suit and sneakers in St Tropez and super-chic Parisian Caroline de Maigret in Isabel Marant jacket and jeans. The French model and music producer has that fabulous Jane Birkin joie de vivre, that easy-going approach to style.

A random stock-take tells me that, I've amassed over 20pairs of trainers (most of which are living in the bathroom): some hi-tech, some old school, some older than Cara Delevingne. But I can't help feeling a little uneasy when sneakers step off the sports field and onto the runway. Over 700 quid for a pair of trainers, do me a favour. When it comes to sneaker style, it should simply be a question of sport. I may have moved on from my not-so-glad-to-wear Gola days to fancy Liberty-print Nike Air Max, but high-end designers, you know where you can stick your overpriced kicks.

DON'T FORGET YOUR SUNGLASSES

Golden Age Hollywood movie stars initially wore sunglasses to protect their eyes from the bright lights on set, and this inadvertently gave them an air of mysterious cool. Wearing shades equated with being a superstar. Anna Wintour uses the same argument when sitting on the front row, today. I'm not a stranger to this prime position (although I'm usually shunted to the back at catwalk shows) and can confirm that it's not exactly retina-scorching. Whether used as a glamorous 'I want to be alone' defence mechanism, to add movie star glamour or simply shade the eyes, sunglasses have become a modern-day necessity. Day and night, indoors and out. I find the older I get, the more I wear mine – and not in a starry fashion. For practical purposes, like: hiding tired eyes and wrinkles, instead of make-up for a quick trip to the local shops and to maintain a sliver of anonymity when making a rare appearance on the blog. If I do post a picture of myself online, I'm either in the distance, wearing sunglasses, or both. And for these handy face-saving uses, I'd class sunglasses as a grown-up style staple. Though I wouldn't recommend wearing them indoors or at night; with failing eyesight that's going to end in tears.

Sunglasses are one of those items that are regularly given out to journalists as press gifts – or what Mr *That's Not My Age* likes to call bribes – and so I have quite a few pairs. Nevertheless, on a friend's 50th birthday weekend, I forgot to pack a pair and had to nip into Poundstretcher for a quick fix. Like a budget Jackie O, I came out with a big pair of bug-eye shades that lasted about five minutes until the cheap lenses made my eyes hurt. Squinting in the sun was less painful. And the moral of that story is: don't leave packing till the last minute and do buy decent lenses.

THREE DIFFERENT SUNGLASSES STYLES:

1. The classic – Whenever a student mentions Audrey Hepburn I want to kill myself, so please forgive the hypocrisy and allow me this one tired reference. *Breakfast at Tiffany's* is 54 years old and Ray-Ban Wayfarers still feel modern today (though the bizarrely racist Mickey Rooney character definitely does not). Two words: timeless style. See also Ray-Ban and Cutler and Gross for Aviators, and Persol. As with Ray-Ban, the Italian brand was originally used for protection by pilots and the military and later adopted by movie stars like Greta Garbo and Steve McQueen, who famously wore the folding PO 714 SM model in *The Thomas Crown Affair*.

2. The kooky – How much did we love the Advanced Stylistas modelling in that fabulous 2013 Karen Walker ad campaign? Ditto Helena Bonham Carter on the red carpet in a pair of show-stopping crystal and filigree Dolce & Gabbana shades and a strapless couture gown. Every season Miu Miu's covetable frames are decorated with swirls or flowers or something equally fabulous. So much better than wearing purple with a red hat, don't you think?

3. The retro – There are certain vintage-inspired designs that never go out of style: curvy cat's eye and fifties 'brow line' shapes, oversized Jackie O frames (with proper lenses) and anything that makes you look like you've just stepped out of a black-and-white Fellini film. And coloured frames can work on grown-ups. I'm not talking about Ye-Ye girls yellow, but eternally chic hues like navy, pale blues and greys, racing green and tortoise shell. For the best retro sunglasses go straight to: Cutler and Gross, Linda Farrow, Ray-Ban and Oliver Peoples.

AND THREE TIPS:

1. Don't wear wraparounds. Ever.

2. Make sure sunglasses fit properly and are proportional to your face size.

3. If you've paid designer prices, try not to sit on them.

SIX STYLISH SPORTS SHOE MOMENTS

1

A SEVEN MONTHS' PREGNANT NENEH CHERRY PERFORMING 'BUFFALO STANCE' ON *TOP OF THE POPS* IN 1988
She wore a metallic Jean Paul Gaultier jacket and matching bra top with a gold medallion the size of a dinner plate round her neck, Ra-Ra skirt over leggings and a pair of Adidas hi-tops. Brilliant.

2

PHOEBE PHILO ON THE CÉLINE CATWALK
and in real life, pairing minimalist chic with New Balance/Nike Air Max/Adidas Stan Smith trainers. Whatever Philo is wearing on her feet, the fashion world will soon follow suit.

3

JANE BIRKIN IN CONVERSE CHUCK TAYLOR CANVAS SNEAKERS: THEN AND NOW
The actress/singer/style icon has said, 'I feel most comfortable in an old pair of jeans, Converse and a man's jersey.'

4

FARRAH FAWCETT'S SKATEBOARD CHASE FOR A 1976 EPISODE OF *CHARLIE'S ANGELS*
wearing a red blouson, Jordache flared jeans and Nike Cortez. Was it the real FF on the skateboard? Do we really care?

5

JENNA LYONS GOES FOR SLICK TOMBOY STYLE AT THE NEW YORK PREMIERE OF *BLUE JASMINE*, 2013
The creative director specialises in the high-low look: J. Crew navy tuxedo, white vest top and Givenchy skate shoes. Perfect.

6

AN EARLY-1990S KATE MOSS, JUST BEFORE SHE STARTED DATING JOHNNY DEPP
and way before she had the misfortune to meet that loser Pete Doherty, looking beautiful in a black maxi dress, black opaque tights, denim jacket and red suede Adidas Gazelles.

Iris Apfel

THE 95-YEAR-OLD STAR NEW YORKER WITH A PENCHANT FOR ACCESSORIES HAS A SERIES OF BOOKS, EXHIBITIONS AND DOCUMENTARIES DEDICATED TO HER MAXIMALIST, BOHEMIAN STYLE.

'If you don't know who you are and you copy someone else's style, then that's sad. You must learn who you are and dress to suit your personality.'

ON BEING A GERIATRIC STARLET

My husband Carl and I think it's funny and ridiculous. I can't get over it. I'm not doing anything different, I've been doing the same thing for years, so I don't know how it happened. Maybe people just caught up …

ON THE FASHION INDUSTRY'S OBSESSION WITH YOUTH

There are a lot of attractive, older women who dress well and yet the shops are full of designs for young things. Apparel producers are really quite mad, the bulk of women with expendable income are over 60 and yet they still use 16-year-old models. It's a stupid run-around. People are starting to put money behind the older market – I can see it's beginning to trickle down, but they should do it more in cosmetics. Using young models with flawless skin and retouching them so that they look like angels; older women know they can never look like that and it annoys them.

ON AGE

Old age is treated like a dreadful disease. I have friends that I've known for years who won't tell me how old they are, it's ridiculous. I never care how old anyone is. I don't know why women are afraid of it – you don't need to look like an old hag. And I don't know why people look in the mirror all the time and worry about their wrinkles, it's so narcissistic. If they spent the same amount of time putting things into their brains as into their faces, they'd be much more interesting.

ON STYLE

Being comfortable is the most important thing – and I don't mean slobby! I never pay attention to trends, if something's in fashion and I look like a horse's ass in it then why would I buy it? It's hard work getting to know yourself – the biggest fashion faux pas is to look in the mirror and see someone else. You need to know your faults and your assets. Style can't be bought or learnt, it's innate. Some people have it, some people don't. Some people are opera singers, some people aren't …

ON STAYING CURRENT

I love museums and the arts, they're very important to me. I always try to stay current and be interested in things, if not you just dry up. If I wasn't designing or doing creative things, I'd go mad. You must get out there and get involved – otherwise you're still living in the dark ages.

ON BEING A NONAGENARIAN

Luckily it's a blessing. At this point a good many of my older friends have gone, but I have lots of younger friends and contemporaries who keep me busy. I don't know why people bitch about it; aches and pains come with the territory, but I never complain, nobody wants to hear that.

ON WHAT YOU'D SAY TO YOUR 15-YEAR-OLD SELF

I don't think that I've changed a lot. I've just matured and progressed. Like any intelligent person, my politics have changed. Lots of people become more conservative as they get older, but I've become more liberal. I'm not a bleeding heart, but if two guys want to get married then let them get married. If somebody wants an abortion, let them have an abortion.

Ruth Chapman

CO-FOUNDER OF BRITISH RETAIL
BRAND AND ONLINE BOUTIQUE
MATCHESFASHION.COM

'I don't mind being older at all. For me it's all about health and vitality and feeling really well; that makes a huge difference.'

**ON BEING A GLOBAL ONLINE
BRAND DIRECTOR**

It's fun. I get more and more confident
about what we're doing all the time. We
went online eight years ago and it's grown
very organically. I was very happy when
we were just retail, but our customers
were travelling all over the world and it
made sense that they could shop with
us when they weren't in London. Things
change constantly and we have to keep on
top of it but I try to make sure that work
doesn't impact on my family life. I'm very
conscious of it and always make an effort
to have a balanced lifestyle.

ON AGE

We've used Linda Rodin (see page 58) in
our campaigns, and I am very inspired by
women who look like that.

ON RUTH CHAPMAN-STYLE

I'd like to say effortless, simple, slightly
masculine. I live in separates and flat
shoes, and I know it sounds ancient and
a bit of an old lady thing but comfort is
important. Having the right amount of
layers. I'm travelling a lot and don't want
to be too hot or too cold.

**ON WHAT WOULD IMPROVE THE
QUALITY OF LIFE**

More sleep, more rest – if I could figure
that out it would be amazing.

ON THE OLD LADY REVOLUTION

I think it's brilliant. It really inspires
younger girls, so they don't have a
sense that it's over by a certain age. It
gives them more choice; they know that

their career can change, they can be a polymath, have kids, do whatever they want to do.

ON WHAT'S IMPORTANT

A good balance between work, life, friends and fun; laughter is very important. I also think being kind to people is important and that kindness shows in people's faces. It's something we should learn very early on.

ON STYLE

Looking modern really is key, but it's not about chasing trends, it's about finding your own DNA; knowing what suits you and sticking with it – but looking around at what's happening and freshening the look.

ON WHAT THE GROWN-UP CUSTOMER WANTS

Value per wear is important. There was a time when we used to sell very expensive dresses for events but now our customers want timelessness. They want great pieces that work back and have different lives in their wardrobe. Pieces that can be put together in different ways.

ON WHAT YOU'D SAY TO YOUR 15-YEAR-OLD SELF

Teens have a tough time. You're never sure of what you want and you don't believe in yourself. I'd say relax. Just chill out a bit, it's all going to be all right. Figure out what you want and go for it.

THE GROWN-UP
STYLE TRIBES

During my early magazine days I was responsible for collating a monthly news page. This involved calling in trannies (film transparencies not cross-dressers, though that would've been fun) that took days to arrive, in the post. Fashion was a rarefied world, where access to PRs and information was done via expensive trade directories and entrance to catwalk shows was seriously restricted. Now it takes a nanosecond for a jpeg to appear in your inbox, everyone has a website and shows are streamed live online. Access to vast quantities of information and product is just a click away. And with all of this on tap, being told that this season we'll be wearing 60s Sportswear or Sophisticated Folklore or whatever (insert silly trend suggestion here), feels quite ridiculous. When we can buy what we want instantly, anytime, day or night, trends have become irrelevant. Now it's all about style.

Style Tribes have always fascinated me: from the punks of my teenage years to the women of *Advanced Style*. I do think that it's human nature to identify with others – with people who dress alike, who appreciate the same things and have similar attitudes and beliefs – whatever your age. Some people may steadfastly stick to one particular look, others might join a different tribe every day of the week. Personally, I like to mix things up. I have a sort of Split-Personality Style: half minimal, menswear-inspired dressing, half bohemian, hippy-punk – with the occasional older and bolder moment thrown in. And I think as we continue to reinvent ourselves throughout our lives, most women have become more comfortable with this high-low, pick and mix approach. Style is a work in progress, being an individual means doing your own thing. But then, having said that, don't we all love to feel part of a grown-up gang?

THE CASUAL GLAMOURPUSS

Face it: most of us wear daywear most of the time. Red Carpet Dressing isn't much use at the coalface and most evenings I'd rather be at home with the Blog Widower and a boxset, anyway. But I do like to think that if a last-minute invitation suddenly pings into my inbox, I'm ready for action. No faffing, no changing, no nonsense. My ideal outfit is good for running around in, morning, noon and night. I call this phenomenon Casual Glamour: a relaxed blend of day and eveningwear, an effortless look that goes everywhere. It's my modus operandi and it's the modern way. Reliable everyday basics are the building blocks of the Casual Glamourpuss's wardrobe – a simple tunic dress, a favourite pair of jeans, a cashmere sweater. But without the drama, you're left looking more 1970s office block than Zaha Hadid swoosh. So, bring on the showbiz staple; this is not any one particular garment, more of a contemporary sartorial sensation – a look-at-me standout piece. Visible in the fine collection of Lurex knitwear and vintage beaded tops I've stockpiled over the years. It's the trashy seaside town in me … that deep-rooted, end-of-the-pier sparkle is hard to shake off. And who wants to lose the magic?

In the fashion world, shimmer and shine, animal print and embellishment have become year-round staples, deployed to add oomph to a simple, everyday outfit. J. Crew's Jenna Lyons is the goddess of Casual Glamour; she's a brilliant stylist as well as a top-notch creative director and puts outfits together in a thoroughly inspirational way. Lyons knows how to mix things up: think diamanté and denim, khaki and leopard print, sequins and stripes. Adding a little bling to the basics is the key to achieving low-key style with an elegant twist. As Ruth Chapman, co-founder and chief executive of Matches Fashion and another icon of the low-key look confirms when we meet, 'I am very drawn to pieces that are quite artisanal and blingy, but I downplay them with a very normcore look. I don't think people dress up any more, it's more low-key than that. Conversational pieces that are quite flashy, or have elements of vulgarity at first glance, are worn in an irreverent way and become more laid-back.'

All of which is good news – who doesn't have something sparkly languishing at the back of their closet? Adding the latest, well-cut wardrobe essentials will give what you already have a modern edge. Throw on an eye-catching metallic jacket with a simple black shirt and cigarette pants. Wear a sequined pencil skirt with a T-shirt and razor-sharp blazer. The go-anywhere appeal of this dressed-up daywear is what the grown-up Glamourpuss loves.

THE ESSENTIALS: A leopard-print coat, jeans in every available colour and wash, sequined pencil skirt, grey marl T-shirt, denim shirt, metallic leather ankle boots, Birkenstock Arizonas, printed or brocade trousers, pimped-up sneakers.

WHERE TO FIND CASUAL GLAMOUR: Isabel Marant, J. Crew, Gap, APC, Whistles, Cedric Charlier, DVF, Penelope Chilvers, Tucker, Bella Freud, Sophia Webster, Michael Kors, proper vintage.

THE STYLE HEROINES:
Fashion editors Renata Molho, Julia Sarr-Jamois and Shala Monroque; Lulu Kennedy Linda Rodin, Ellen von Unwerth, Bella Freud, Grace Coddington, Alison Goldfrapp, Thelma Speirs, and, of course, Jane Birkin.

THE OLDER AND
BOLDER BRIGADE

'The whole idea of shifting the view towards older women is quite anarchic. If you're looking for punk rock, look at *Advanced Style*,' says Simon Doonan, Creative Director of Barney's, at the beginning of the documentary on Ari Seth Cohen's street style blog. And he has a point. Sue Kreitzman's Old Lady Revolution feels like a proper rebellious movement. Fashion freedom fighters like Iris Apfel, Linda Rodin and Beatrix Ost are styling it out on the streets of New York, not sitting at home in elasticated waist slacks and slippers. Though, as Iris Apfel points out, a lot of these women have been dressing this way for decades. It's just that now the trend has gone global, there's been an acceptance of bohemian outsiders, artists and designers; women like Molly Parkin, Zandra Rhodes and Vivienne Westwood have gone from freak to chic.

The Older and Bolder Brigade celebrate life with equal measures of energy and eye-popping accessories. These women are confident, creative and they care about how they look. This flamboyant peacock style is all about individuality and enjoyment. 'It's not vanity, ' Ari Seth Cohen tells me, 'They're doing it for themselves because it makes them feel good and lifts the spirits.' He goes on to explain how he is inundated with emails from women of all ages inspired by his photographs and the prospect of growing older – he was once chased through the New York subway by a gang of devoted fans: English pensioners (Hell's Grannies?), in search of an Advanced Style appearance.

'This collective spirit has led to an inter-generational appreciation for all things age-related,' adds Ari, 'This pro-ageing, self-expressive campaign has cracked the surface of traditional lifestyle media and people now acknowledge the fact that older people are not, and should not be invisible.' It might not be everyone's cup of tea, but I think Older and Bolder is bloody brilliant. A gang of pensioners with a punk rock attitude – you can count me in.

OLDER AND BOLDER IN THREE EASY STEPS...

1. TURN ON TO A TURBAN
From Grace Kelly at the 1955 Cannes Film Festival to Zadie Smith in north-west London, the turban has an illustrious style heritage. Try one with a brightly coloured collarless coat, a printed dress or an all-black outfit and a denim jacket. And wave goodbye to bad hair days.

2. PILE ON THE ACCESSORIES
Avoid the everything-but-the-kitchen-sink look by wearing a pared-down outfit and pair of kooky sunglasses (see page 29). Or go for everyday elegance by taking a plain, long-sleeved T-shirt and slinging on a couple of beaded necklaces in the same colour.

3. DON'T BE COLOUR SHY
Take the incremental approach and add bright flashes to a signature look. (See page 23 for How to wear colour without looking like a crazy lady.)

THE STYLE HEROINES:

Grey Gardens' 'Big Edie' and 'Little Edie', all the Advanced Stylistas, fashion stylist Catherine Baba, fashion director Lucinda Chambers, fashion designer Zandra Rhodes, fashion journalist Lynn Yaeger, Helena Bonham Carter (and her mum Elena), Vivienne Westwood, Lulu Guinness, designer Gudrun Sjoden, founder of Kids Company Camilla Batmanghelidjh, singer-songwriter Siouxsie Sioux.

WHERE TO FIND IT:

Prada, Zara, Clover Canyon, Cos, Marni, Boden, H&M, Markus Lupfer, MSGM, Moschino, Vivienne Westwood, Dries Van Noten, proper vintage, everywhere.

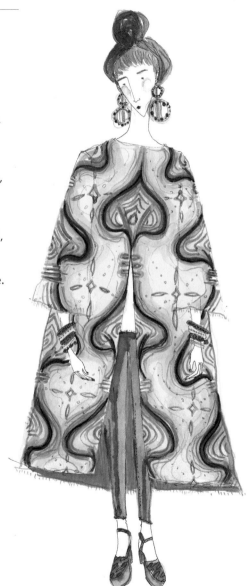

THE SUPERPOWER
DRESSER

The high-flying businesswoman no longer feels the need to barge her way into the boardroom with a chunk of fabric on each shoulder the size of a Cameo codpiece. Now that we've finally chipped the glass ceiling, it's all about dressing to please ourselves in a powerful, modern way. Next on the agenda: equal pay and representation, but that's another book. 'Women have developed more of a sense of personal style as they are feeling more confident in senior positions,' says Kim Winser, founder of online fashion label Winser London, who has an impressive track record, including stints as CEO of Pringle of Scotland and global president and CEO of Aquascutum. 'A decade ago, women were still breaking through and trying so hard. This was often reflected in their chosen outfits – which were perhaps a little too influenced by a man's sense of dressing, too formal and structured.'

Superpower Dressers like Apple's Angela Ahrendts, Christine Lagarde, Sheryl Sandberg and Michelle Obama are in control of their lives as well as their wardrobes. Talking of control, arbiter of style Anna Wintour is never less than impeccable in designer frock, kitten heels and don't-mess-with-me sunglasses.

Fashion tastemakers Linda Fargo (senior vice-president of Bergdorf Goodman), Joan Burstein (co-founder of Browns fashion) and retail guru Mary Portas all tend to stick to simple shapes – a shift or tunic dress, a pussy-bow blouse

and sharp trousers – and play around with colour and texture. When we meet, Kim Winser is wearing slinky wide-leg trousers, heels and a simple cashmere sweater. 'I like to feel stylish, comfortable and confident,' she comments. 'My clothes allow me to be flexible; on very busy days, I can wear them all day long and still feel great at dinner.'

The Superpower Dresser's signature look is always polished and professional. Style is part of her DNA. You know what you're going to get – and that means she can get down to business. 'Investing in quality wardrobe essentials makes a serious difference,' Kim continues, 'And these items are likely to be worn more often than an expensive evening dress – luxurious fabrics and the perfect cut are the most important factors. Keeping the accessory in tune with the outfit is key. Don't let it take over. Keep the look well-balanced.' Whether chairing a board meeting or travelling the globe, the aim is to add personality to the basics while remaining cool, calm and collected: 'It's important to add your own style and not look overdone,' points out Kim. 'Think cosmetics here; the best look is when you look like you haven't really bothered but actually you have carefully accentuated your features using excellent product.'

And the death of occasionwear … Walking past Buckingham Palace at the end of a summer's day, I was confronted by hordes of Queen's Garden Party guests spilling out onto the street. I gawped in dismay. This was an occasionwear debacle like no other; a horror show of florals, frou-frou and revolting fascinators. I felt like I'd died and gone to Alexon. If you want my advice on dressing for special occasions, it's this: don't buy anything new. Occasionwear is dead. Spend money on a blow-dry not a blow-out. Take inspiration from the Superpower Dressers and take the less-is-better approach – the simple jewel-coloured shift dress, necklace and kitten heel combination is smart, simple and easy to replicate.

WHERE TO FIND SUPERPOWER STYLE:

Chanel, Jaeger, Issa, LK Bennett, Mary Katrantzou, Hobbs, Goat, Cos, Diane Von Fürstenburg, Roksanda, Osman, Sophie D'Hoore, Zara, Jil Sander, Winser London, Nicholas Kirkwood.

THE ESSENTIALS:

The pussy-bow blouse, the leather dress, wide-leg trousers in primary colours, the blazer, the white shirt, the printed pencil skirt, the pointed shoe (heeled and flat), the power necklace, the regular blow-dry, the chauffeur.

THE GENTLEWOMAN

An elegant, grown-up tomboy with discerning taste, a love of culture and an eye for detail: meet The Gentlewoman. Her look is pared-down, modern, a blend of masculine and feminine. Think off-duty Cate Blanchett, Tilda Swinton in a tux, Jenna Lyons wearing J. Crew and Céline. 'It's an overall state of mind. Someone who is considered, not just about the way they look, but the whole package,' says journalist and author of *How to be a Modern Gentlewoman* Navaz Batliwalla. 'It's someone who cares about design, technique and craft, the finer things in life.' But The Gentlewoman isn't just a tomboy in Céline – though the brand's designer Phoebe Philo is her ultimate style heroine, 'Her clothes don't have to be expensive, just well made and long lasting. Whether it's a Gap T-shirt or a pair of Church's shoes, the design will be considered, the proportions are right, there is a functionality that is also beautiful to look at, feel or hold.'

From Goodyear-welted brogues to average weft-count, attention to every last detail is key, 'There is definitely a bit of the research-a-holic geek in there,' adds Navaz, 'Knowing the provenance of something and using it for years because the quality is great and you love it, rather than because so-and-so celebrity endorsed it.' And now that we've had our landfill of fast fashion, this background knowledge is the thing. The whole procedure is carefully weighed up beforehand; there are no rash decisions here. 'Gentlewomen are careful, conscious consumers, not raging shopaholics. They like nice things but don't consume for the sake of having a "must-buy".'

When it comes to designing The Gentlewoman's wardrobe, it's all about wearability, fabric and cut. As creative director of fashion label Studio Nicholson Nick Wakeman says, 'Everything must go with everything, so I stick to a colour palette of black, white, pale blue and khaki and keep buying wardrobe repeats. When you keep it this simple, fabric and texture become really important. I like playing with proportions to add interest, but you have to get the fit just right. Look for trousers that fall gently from the hip that don't grip. Have a few shirt buttons undone, play with what god gave you. I think that relaxed tomboy style is really sexy.' Nick regularly looks to vintage menswear for inspiration, 'I wear a lot of men's shirts and jackets, as a rule I have a much stronger emotional response to menswear than womenswear. I find the detailing in menswear is so much more considered.' Though an element of surprise is important too, 'I like the Italian phrase *spezzato*. It's used to describe menswear that's not quite matching or a little "off". Having a little quirk like a scarf under a jacket and no shirt. That idea of playing around is quite British too.'

Clothes are just a small part of the elegant tomboy's carefully curated lifestyle. When she's not obsessing over the perfect white T-shirt, she's at an art gallery private view, or watching Kirsty Wark on BBC *Newsnight*, riding a horse or reading her favourite magazine: *The Gentlewoman*, of course.

THE ESSENTIALS:

The mannish shirt, the cashmere sweater, a man's watch, the white T-shirt, the Chelsea boot, rolled-up chinos, brogues, a navy overcoat, Levi's 501s, Ray-Ban Aviators.

THE STYLE HEROINES:

Sofia Coppola, Amelia Earhart, Margaret Howell, Penny Martin, Katharine Hepburn, fashion consultant Yasmin Sewell, actress Maxine Peake, fashion director Tonne Goodman, designer Andrée Putman, artist Polly Morgan and singer Pauline Black.

WHERE TO FIND IT:

Paul Smith, Céline, Cos, Toast, Studio Nicholson, Sunspel, Margaret Howell, APC, John Smedley, Gap, Church's, ESK cashmere, Everlane, Theory, Tabitha Simmons.

'Style is knowing who you are, what you want to say, and not giving a damn.'

– Orson Welles

THE FABULOUS FEMME

'The first thing to do is to arrange to be born in Paris,' Diana Vreeland once announced. 'After that, everything follows quite naturally.' Now that there are so many books and blogs on French Style, there's really no need to be born there, we can all pretend. And while we know that not every Parisian woman looks like Inès de la Fressange (just as not every Londoner looks like Kate Moss), there is an allure about Parisian Chic, a certain *Je ne sais quoi* that makes it more popular than the Ladurée boutique at Christmas. 'It's attitude, confidence and nonchalance,' says Paris-based journalist, and author of *Forever Chic*, Tish Jett. 'French women always look comfortable, even in sky-high heels walking over cobbles. They dress to please themselves, they know what suits them and their clothes fit.'

The Fabulous Femme has a style confidence that comes from sticking to perennial classics rather than following fashion fads: Carine Roitfeld practically lives in a silk Equipment shirt, it's always a kick-ass jacket for Farida Khelfa, (brand ambassador for the house of Schiaparelli) and cigarette pants for Emmanuelle Alt. And this is why we all love a little faux Français, we're enamoured by *une femme d'un certain âge* who confidently sticks to what she knows, and she knows what suits.

Maybe I've got chic for brains, but I also think it helps living in a country where women aren't chucked on the scrapheap as soon as they turn 40. From the head of the IMF to the icons of French cinema, it would seem that on the other side of the Channel, women are revered throughout their lives, not just during the reproductive years. Our Gallic friends aren't interested in trying to look younger or in showing acres of flesh in a 'do my tits look big in this?' way. 'It's about being sensual not sexy,' adds Tish, 'I don't ever recall seeing a French woman trying to look sexy. They'll have one more button unbuttoned, but it doesn't come off as aggressive, just soft and natural.'

But although we'd like to believe it comes naturally, we know that effortless style does require effort. That an understated outfit hasn't been thrown together in five minutes flat and the Fabulous Femme's beauty regime isn't just a walk around the washbasin. Nonetheless, the overall impression of French Style is fluency. It looks so easy-breezy, which is why it's so appealing. There is a certain confidence that comes from dressing to please yourself and being pleased with the way you dress – an ease of being.

HOW TO LOOK FRENCH EVEN WHEN YOU'RE NOT:

DON'T FOLLOW TRENDS

French women aren't fashion victims. They like to keep it clean and simple; think Catherine Deneuve's lifelong addiction to the Yves Saint Laurent tuxedo, ditto Françoise Hardy and the leather biker jacket. Don't try too hard. Don't complicate it. Don't mess with frills. *C'est tout.*

PLAY WITH ACCESSORIES

Though we'd all love a Louis Vuitton bag, a pair of Roger Vivier shoes and Hermès scarf in our armoire, the good thing about accessories is that they don't have to cost a fortune. Pile on the beads and bangles like Loulou de la Falaise, wear a scarf like Christine Lagarde or just experiment *un peu* and do your own thing. But, never, ever buy matching shoes and handbag.

SPEND TIME ON YOURSELF...

Admittedly, this is not a very British thing – we apply make-up on the commute, we don't have a dermatologist on speed-dial – but spending time on a more effective beauty regime and a more streamlined wardrobe will add a little French polish.

BUT DON'T LET IT LOOK LIKE YOU DO

Keep the hair slightly tousled, let the oversized men's shirt hang loose at the back, the overall impression should be one of not being too 'done'. It works for Charlotte Rampling and Jane Birkin.

THE STYLE HEROINES:

Models Caroline de Maigret and Farida Khelfa; Christine Lagarde, Clemence Poesy, Ines de la Fressange, Catherine Deneuve, Emmanuelle Alt, founder of Bonpoint Marie-France Cohen, Coco Chanel, Françoise Hardy, fashion photographer and illustrator Garance Doré.

WHERE TO FIND IT:

Sandro, Merci, Sonia Rykiel, American Vintage, Chanel, Iro, Joseph, Petit Bateau, Agnes b, APC, Aimé, Zadig et Voltaire, Equipment, Comptoir des Cotonniers.

THE SCANDINISTA

The Fabulous Femme needs to keep on her Vivier-clad toes, there's some cool competition blowing in from northern Europe. The Scandinista has her own laid-back style, her own fashion week (Stockholm) and an array of fabulous home-grown brands to choose from. As with French Style, this type of understated elegance is popular worldwide; not least in the United States where 'Hamptons Chic meets the Kennedy's in Martha's Vineyard' is not a million miles away from the Summerhouse-on-the-Stockholm-archipelago vibe. A strong connection harks back to the 19th century when Swedish and Norwegian immigration reached its peak, and is evident again in the number of Scandinavian designers and fashion bloggers popping up across the pond in New York.

I've always felt like a secret Scandinavian; the lifestyle, the fjords, the beautiful design – maybe it's a Viking heritage? After all, I do get regularly mistaken for a local when on tour. I have braved the Norwegian Arctic Circle in winter, cycled around Copenhagen in spring and swum in the B-B-B-Baltic (it was bloody freezing, even in July). So this new mood is right up my *gade*. 'I've never been big at dressing up,' admits Tove Westling, the Stockholm-born, London-based owner of Varg PR (a company representing Scandinavian brands in the UK), during one of our regular conversations on superior Scandi Style, 'I think a beautiful, simple, clean kind of piece speaks for itself and gives a much cooler impression than something that screams "look at me".' And this calm northern European persona is nothing new; Hollywood stars Greta Garbo and Ingrid Bergman were too cool for stage school, not to mention Anita Ekberg who left Scandinavia for Italy and *La Dolce Vita*. And strong female characters have played a starring role in Nordic Noir TV thrillers *The Killing*, *The Bridge* and *Borgen* – as well as in real-life politics where 67-year-old Gudrun Schyman is leader of the Swedish Feminist Initiative Party and the Danish prime minister, Helle Thorning-Schmidt, is the equivalent of *Borgen*'s Birgitte Nyborg.

Unafraid to play around with masculine and feminine silhouettes, the Scandinista loves mannish jackets and coats, minimal shapes, neutral colours and natural fabrics. 'I think it relates to the way we are consuming nowadays,' Tove continues, 'People want sustainability and pieces that last, rather than fast fashion that needs to be replaced every six months. Even though many Scandi designers have a very different artistic expression, what they tend to have in common is a contemporary feel, clean lines and a way of putting styles together that doesn't date.' But it's not all boyfriend jackets and shades of greige, The Scandinista has an innate fondness for nautical stripes, patterned knitwear and beautiful bright prints. Which brings me full circle: in 1960, Jackie Kennedy bought a selection of affordable cotton sundresses from a Marimekko stockist in Cape Cod. After being criticised for spending too much money on Parisian designer fashion, she was then complimented on her thrift.

THE STYLE HEROINES:

The band First Aid Kit, Crown Princess Mary of Denmark, Saga Norén (*The Bridge*), Helena Christensen, Carolyn Bessett-Kennedy, Ruth Chapman, Sarah Lund (*The Killing*), bloggers Elin Kling, Pernille Teisbaek and Hanna Steffanson.

WHERE TO FIND SCANDI STYLE:

Day Birger et Mikkelsen, Cos, Acne, H&M, Cheap Monday, Bruuns Bazaar, Swedish Hasbeens, Skandium, &Other Stories, Filippa K, Monki, Ann Sofie-Back, Dagmar, Gudrun & Gudrun, Whyred.

THE AGELESS ROCKER

'Look out you rock 'n' rollers, pretty soon now you're gonna get older,' warned David Bowie in 1971, and inevitably we all did. But 44 years later, musicians like Patti Smith, Marianne Faithfull, Françoise Hardy and Chrissie Hynde are still rolling on. As fans of what I like to call Rock Chickery; mannish tailoring, military gear, the leather biker jacket and black skinny pants, they are growing older with dignity and style and a wardrobe full of effortlessly cool clothes. These are women who do their own thing regardless of what's popular. Their look is timeless, trend-defying and so chic that Carine Roitfield, Emmanuelle Alt and the French *Voguettes* can't get enough of it. All mussed-up hair, men's shirts, leather trousers and black boots.

These elements of rock and roll style, are now part of our everday wardrobe. There's a great Andy Warhol quote that sums the phenomenon up perfectly: 'When a person is the beauty of their day, and their looks are really in style, and then the times change, and 10 years go by, if they keep exactly their same look and don't change anything and if they take care of themselves, they'll still be a beauty. You have to hang on in periods when your style isn't popular, because if it's good, it'll come back and you'll be recognised as a beauty once again.'

So. Hang on to yourself. Hang on to your style. You're never too old to rock and roll.

ROCKING OUT NOT ROCKING CHAIR: THE GROWN-UP GUIDE TO GIGS

I may be closer to 60 than 20, but as a lifelong music lover I'm never going to stop going to gigs. Ever. Though it's not as easy as it used to be. First, there's the ticketing conundrum to contend with. Having more money than your teenage self means that the extortionate price is not a problem, finding time to book tickets for the latest hip band and then be around for the Ticketmaster courier is. And when you do manage to drag your weary bones to the online ticket office, the tendency is to opt for bands playing venues with seats. So that's Bryan Adams in an enormodome, or some jazz. Nice. Mr *That's Not My Age* has taken me to a couple of jazz concerts; being part of a sophisticated, older crowd feels very grown-up, but I can never work out whether the rows of nodding grey heads are getting into the groove or dropping off.

Standing in a dark room with flashing strobe lights and banging tunes doesn't have the same appeal when you're stone cold sober and tired and have to get up for work in the morning.

The key here is to drink lots of caffeine. Start with coffee and move on to a bottled beer with a Diet Coke chaser. You'll soon feel so bloated you won't want to drink any more, or dance. Dancing is another problem the over-40s have to contend with. So, gently does it. Stick to an inoffensive sway, avoid the full-blown dad dance and do not, under any circumstances, wave a lighter/smart phone in the air.

Next, find a quiet spot. Drunken youths with no spatial awareness can make the grown-up gig-goer grumpy. So try to ignore them and settle down somewhere between the mixing desk and the merchandise stand. Don't forget, if you intend to stay for the encore, comfy shoes are a must and should you find yourself queuing for that garish band T-shirt, it's time to go home.

THE STYLE HEROINES:
Yoko Ono, Debbie Harry, Kate Moss, fashioner designer Pam Hogg, punk icon Soo Catwoman, former model and muse Betty Catroux, Lou Doillon, Grace Jones, Alison Mosshart, Stella Tennant, Skin (Skunk Anansie), musicians Kim Gordon, Viv Albertine and Joan Jett.

WHERE TO BUY IT:
All Saints, Ann Demeulemeester, army surplus stores, Saint Laurent Paris, Rick Owens, Topshop, Shrimps, Zadig & Voltaire, Isabel Marant, Vivienne Westwood, Acne, The Kooples, J Brand.

'Be yourself. Everyone else is already taken!'
– Oscar Wilde

WHAT I'VE LEARNT ABOUT FASHION

1

EVERY OUTFIT NEEDS ONE SHOWBIZ ITEM

A standout piece to perk things up; something that you'll want to wear till it falls apart. Think maximum impact, minimum effort.

2

DON'T WASTE MONEY ON SHIT CLOTHES

There's no need for all this careless consumerism – and who has the space to store a never-ending supply of new stuff anyway. Keeping it chic is all about simplicity (see Emmanuelle Alt, Phoebe Philo et al). Experiment with what you have already or take the buy less, buy better approach.

3

OCCUPY THE MIDPOINT ON THE DAY/EVENING VENN DIAGRAM OF STYLE

Don't save anything for best. It's all about 24-hour Casual Glamour now.

4

SLING THE SPANX

I've never worn them. Never will. To me, control knickers are an object of torture, like girdles and corsets before them. Yes, they're designed to make women look thinner. But what do we want? Freedom for grown-ups!

5

BUY FRENCH LINGERIE AND REPLACE IT REGULARLY

A skanky grey bra is a step too far.

6

AVOID MATCHY-MATCHY

Looking too coordinated or try-hard appears dated. The aim is to look effortless, modern and fresh. Mix it up.

7

WEAR WHAT YOU LIKE

Things you always feel right in. You're going to be a FABster for a very long time so it's best to choose clothes that make you feel happy, comfortable and confident.

8

IGNORE THE RULES

As Marilyn Monroe said, 'If I'd observed all the rules, I'd never have got anywhere.'

9

TAKE YOUR SHIRTS TO THE CLEANERS

This is something I picked up off Manhattan Brother. After spending years perfecting the 'front-only' ironing technique, the grab-and-go potential of a freshly laundered shirt feels like a natural progression.

10

SPEND MONEY ON DECENT SHOES

Your feet are worth it.

Linda Rodin

MEET THE FABULOUS NEW YORK STYLIST WITH AN EPONYMOUS SKINCARE RANGE AND A BURGEONING CAREER AS A FASHION MODEL.

'One of my friends gave me some good advice: forget about the wrinkles and focus on the silhouette.'

ON AGE

To me, 66 is not even old. Two of my best friends are 89 and 91 and they're living their lives and enjoying every day. Ageing isn't easy – it's hard to have wrinkles and to wake up every morning and feel worse than you did a year ago. I'd never have a facelift though, so I guess if wrinkles are my biggest problem then I'm very lucky. Health is the most important thing.

ON BEING AN OLDER MODEL

The modelling thing is fun, it's a gift and so much easier than being a stylist (which means carrying loads of clothes around). I want to say, 'Where were you 40 years ago?!' But the pictures are always retouched, which is depressing. I mean, they retouch 18 year olds – it's just a game.

ON STYLE

I'd describe my style as simple, with a little flare. I like modern clothes. It's about being interesting. I'm not flamboyant. I don't like to be flashy. Bright pink or orange lipstick is as bold as I get. I don't want to be zany, wear kimonos at eight in the morning and 100 Bakelite bracelets. All those women do it as a last hurrah, and that's wonderful but I don't want to be that woman in the stripy socks. I'd rather be Georgia O'Keefe than wackadoo.

ON THE OLD LADY REVOLUTION

Old people have been around forever, so why now? Fashion revolves around money so it's down to economics. I do think it's partially a trend because it seems selective; not all old people are being embraced. It's not those with no teeth who live in Georgia.

ON HAVING FUN

I don't do any exercise but I like to walk a lot with my dog Winky. And though it sounds superficial, I like to go shopping. I'm never going to buy a 5,000 dollar handbag but I'm a stylist and I get a pleasure out of being creative, out of using myself as a canvas.

ON WHAT YOU'D SAY TO YOUR 15-YEAR-OLD SELF

Stop being so insecure, you look wonderful ... all those silly things I laboured over, what a waste of time.

ON STAYING IN

I'm such a homebody, I don't go out much at all – I'm very antisocial in a profound way. I love my apartment, I've been here for 35 years and I love my own space with my dog and stuff. I need my downtime, to collect my thoughts. My 94-year-old friend complained that she never saw me so I said, 'I'd love you to come over.' She came in, looked around and said, 'Now I understand why you never go out.'

Nick Wakeman

THE LONDON-BASED CREATIVE DIRECTOR OF
THE FASHION LABEL STUDIO NICHOLSON. SHE
HAS WORKED IN THE FASHION INDUSTRY FOR
ALMOST 20 YEARS AND DESIGNED FOR THE
LIKES OF DIESEL AND MARKS & SPENCER.

*'When I turned 40, I stopped
giving a fuck. I don't care what
people think of me. I will wear
what I feel amazing in.'*

ON STUDIO NICHOLSON

My grandmother was called Nicholson. She was a very stylish lady so I named my label after her. I feel enormously proud of Studio Nicholson, but not in an arrogant way; I have had incredible support. I have these little quiet moments where I really feel very grateful. I count myself as much more than a fashion designer – that's just a small part of running a brand. The tough bit comes in making the right choices at every step of the way and sticking to your principles and never giving up.

ON GENTLEWOMAN STYLE

It's the pieces that you choose. The button-down Oxford shirt, the Levi's 501s, the white T-shirt (I spend far too long searching for the perfect one) the mac, the grey cashmere sweater. It's that borrowed-from-my-bloke look, even though I don't have a bloke. Maybe I'm pretending!

ON AGE

I spent my 20s not knowing anything, my 30s working it out and I'm going to spend my 40s using what I know. I'm really all right with getting older, more than all right. Worrying about wrinkles is very restrictive; I would say that it's not being free. How you behave is more important than how you look. That's your legacy.

ON CONFIDENCE

On a personal level I've never felt confident, I've always been a bit shy but I'm not scared any more. I have no fear of not being good enough and that confidence translates into how I feel about my looks.

ON DESIGNING

When designing a piece, the three things I keep in mind are grace, elegance and ease.

ON STYLE

Trying too hard is sad; effortless style is much more appealing. Even if you spend four hours getting it right! I like to keep it simple, I want to emphasise the best bits of me and I think if you're underdressed, it plays up what God gave you and people focus on the good bits – like personality! My style is so simple I can get dressed in the dark. It's fuss-free dressing but I can glam it up.

ON WHAT YOU'D SAY TO YOUR 15-YEAR-OLD SELF

Follow your creative instincts and don't stray from the path. I have always been interested in the same things and I think I pretty much saw my creative journey at an early age. I feel like my compass is set straight with Studio Nicholson. There have been a few wrong turns along the way but this feels like me coming home.

Teruko Burrell

LIVES IN SANTA MONICA AND AFTER A CAREER IN THE ARTS, FINALLY REALISED HER DREAM OF BECOMING A MODEL IN HER MID-40S.

'Wisdom comes with age; now I confidently accept my body shape and my big grey hair. This is who I am and what I look like.'

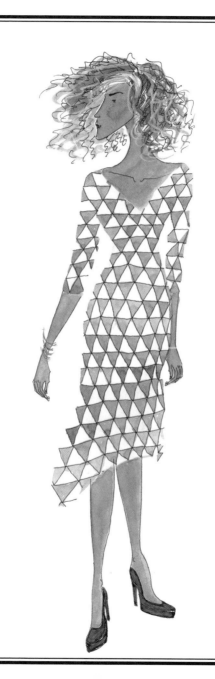

ON MODELLING

I always wanted to model, but in my 20s I never had the courage or the confidence to do so. I remember being in Paris and being incredibly shy when I went to an open call. During my 30s I thought perhaps it wasn't just a childhood dream and something I could possibly pursue, particularly after having my teeth straightened. Finally, in my 40s instead of asking 'why?' I thought 'why not?' and went for it. I'm 56 now and have been modelling for 10 years. I truly enjoy it because I waited so long to pursue it.

ON THE OLD LADY REVOLUTION

I think it's a proper movement. Brands are starting to realise that women our age want to see clothes on women our age – which is good for me because I'm getting more commercial work!

ON STYLE

I love Diane Keaton's style: the tomboyish look, the bowler hats. I'm paired down to the max. Very casual – I love jeans and sensible shoes. I wear minimal make-up, just lip colour and some product in my hair. I'm very low maintenance.

ON MOVING AROUND

I enjoy the arts and the Getty Museum was a great place to work (I was there for 16 years), but there comes a time when you are ready for a career change. I always wanted to live in New York so when I was offered a contract with Wilhelmina Models, I went for it. I thrived on the dynamic energy of New York, but when the tenants moved out of my Santa Monica apartment, during the recession, it was difficult to rent out. I was reluctant to leave New York but decided to move back and now I work more in Los Angeles.

ON RELAXING

I love to exercise. It makes me feel good mentally. I walk lots and run along the beach a couple of times a week. Though I find it easier coming down the stairs than going back up.

ON AGE

I embrace getting older. The only 'work' I've had done is a set of braces on my teeth when I was 35 and laser treatment to correct near-sightedness at 45. I take more chances. I don't take things personally. I take better care of myself (although I need to stretch more!) I am grateful for my health. I treasure kindness. I enjoy wearing stylish loose-fitting clothes that flatter my body – not everything has to be tight fitting.

ON WHAT YOU'D SAY TO YOUR 15-YEAR-OLD SELF

I would say, 'Relax, things have a way of working out and in hindsight you'll see that. Have patience.'

NEVER MIND THE BOTOX

Nora Ephron was right about the increasing maintenance levels as you get older, and I still laugh when I think of her brilliant 'only eight hours a week away from looking like a bag lady' comment. But who has a spare eight hours? When it comes to grooming, I'm pretty low maintenance. My beauty regime takes about five minutes – including make-up, cleansing and moisturising. I don't bother with toner. I've never really seen the point, apart from for photocopying. But one thing I've realised as I've been researching this book, is that as we get older and certainly as we go through the menopause, we need to find time to look after ourselves a bit more. Every single beauty expert I've spoken to has said the same thing, 'Pay attention to yourself.' International make-up artist and beauty expert Ruby Hammer, 53, told me, 'You can't expect someone to pay attention to

you and make you look better when you haven't paid attention to yourself. Take responsibility; at this age we shouldn't be copping out.' And it was at that point I decided it was time to quit my 'face wipes on the bedside cabinet' habit.

> 'I think your whole life shows in your face and you should be proud of that.'
> – Lauren Bacall

There are no miraculous products out there, 'If there was a holy grail of anti-wrinkle creams, we'd all be sleeping in a vat of it,' says Sara Raeburn, beauty expert and make-up artist, but a great skincare regime

really does help. 'I like to take five minutes to be nice to myself,' she says, 'I cleanse, moisturise and massage my face religiously. My skincare routine is somewhere between meditation and boot camp (the only one that is painless, enjoyable and restful); I think of it as mindfulness for the skin.'

My own cobbled-together version of self-maintenance takes a holistic approach to beauty and wellbeing, one that includes coffee and wine – as Oscar Wilde said, 'Everything in moderation, including moderation.' And it's achieved through exercise (swimming, riding a bike, walking, Pilates – which hopefully will lead to running again soon), acupuncture and not looking in the mirror too often. By taking care of the whole package rather than obsessing over tiny details. As the great Iris Apfel says, 'I don't know why people look in the mirror all the time and worry about their wrinkles, it's so narcissistic. If they spent the same amount of time putting things into their brains as into their faces, they'd be much more interesting.'

THE SKIN I'M IN

I don't have a dermatologist, so I was curious to speak to Dr Sam Bunting, a London-based cosmetic dermatologist with a practice on Harley Street and a very busy schedule. 'Skin is the single most powerful asset we have,' Dr Sam tells me. 'We might not be able to get Angelina's lips, but we can make our skin look as healthy as possible.' She then goes on to explain that her approach is to begin with the medical, using active ingredients for correction, and then move onto cosmetic

beautification, like downturned mouth corners and frown lines.

My main concern is sun damage. Things have moved on since the days when I used to lie out on one of my nan's hand-knitted blankets, in our back garden, slathered in coconut oil. Back then we didn't use sunscreen. Luckily there wasn't much sun anyway. Family holidays were usually a quick trip up the M6 to the Lake District in northern England. We would set off at the crack of dawn to miss the traffic – often arriving early at our destination, we'd sit in the car until a cafe opened, we could have a cup of tea and Mum could write the postcards, 'To get them out of the way', before heading to the caravan site. Fortunately we couldn't afford to go to the Mediterranean or things might be worse.

> 'Fighting ageing is like the War on Drugs. It's expensive, does more harm than good and has been proven to never end.'
> – Amy Poehler

Is it any wonder then, that when I started working in my 20s and earned enough for a trip abroad, I went silly for a suntan? And now have the sunspots to prove it. In a closing-the-stable-door type manner, the sunscreen factor I use has

DR SAM BUNTING'S ADVICE ON SKINCARE

1

MODIFY YOU SUN BEHAVIOUR

It's the most important thing you can do.

2

TAKE A HEALTHY APPROACH TO SKINCARE

Making the most of your best feature is far more important than having a face full of filler. (And, as Sam says: 'I may regret saying that as I'll do myself out of a few clients!')

3

EAT 80 PER CENT OF WHAT YOU SHOULD EAT

And 20 per cent of what you want to eat.

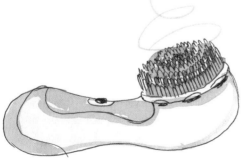

4

HAVE SEX

It gives you a natural glow.

5

MOVE YOUR BODY!

You'll look less tired.

increased with age and knowledge of skin damage. If only I'd taken more care, taken the Cate Blanchett approach and donned a sun hat and rash vest, I might have a lovely luminescent complexion too.

Now. We need to talk about Botox. But let's keep it brief. Research has found that it can make you happier and calmer and alleviate depression. It doesn't make you look younger (and in fact you need less Botox as you get older), it just makes you look less angry, stressed or human.

Whenever I see someone with inflated cheeks or too much botox/filler, it always reminds me of an old house that's had new windows put in that don't quite match the rest of the frontage, and it still looks like an old house. As I've already said, it's a personal choice and not one I'd ever take. I was constantly told to 'Cheer up, love …'by random men throughout my teens and 20s, and when I met Mr *That's Not My Age*, at 39, he thought I was frowning at him (hard to believe he didn't recognise this as The Look of Love), so by now I'm used to how I look. I'm not the Botox police. If you do inject, that's your business, but it's worth taking a minute to think about where the toxins and the money are going. As Dr Sam points out, 'There's only so much you can do about soft tissue – you can't stop the ageing process and you are never going to look the same as you do now in 10 or 20 years' time. Look after yourself, practice good skincare and take a healthy approach to life. It's not rocket science.'

I certainly wouldn't class myself as a skincare expert, but one thing I do know is that there's no need to overload the skin and use 30 different products a day. Keep it simple. All you need is a cleanser, serum (or facial oil), and a moisturiser with SPF. As Jane Cunningham, writer and founder of British Beauty Blogger points out: 'There are a myriad of science claims and some very powerful marketing campaigns designed to part us from our money and wage war against age, but my view is that unless you are super-keen on flinging cash at a promise, you're better off buying beauty products that make you feel happy.'

FACIAL MASSAGE DOES WORK – ASK JULIETTE BINOCHE

Su-Man Hsu is a 51-year-old facialist to the stars, including Frieda Pinto, Juliette Binoche and, er, me. All right, I've seen her three times in three years, but let a woman dream. Whenever La Binoche is filming, she calls upon Su-Man to massage her face for half an hour, every day before the action starts. 'I look like shit at 4 a.m.', points out the London-based therapist (I doubt that, she's stunning), 'but Juliette looks amazing.'

I arrive late for my first appointment, all a-fluster having spent an hour and a half on public transport in 30-degree heat. With sweat dripping from my bare face, hair scraped back, feeling exhausted, grim, and desperate for the loo, I look like Pig Pen. The studio is a haven of Zen-like calm. Su-Man Hsu is charming and serene. Her treatment uses hi-tech, 90 per cent botanical products with active ingredients (a beauty range is now available online). Stripping down to my underwear is a shameful experience; I haven't planned for this and so what I'm wearing is quite shabby. I imagine Juliette Binoche in matching Chantal Thomass lingerie and quickly leap under the covers. Su-Man's massage technique is very firm – not quite pummelling, more of a kneading action 'to work the muscles'. Her fingers dance around the face using a combination of Taiwanese and Japanese techniques and it feels fantastic.

Afterwards, my face does look different. Cheeks are plumper, eyes less saggy/wrinkly round the edges; my whole face has been naturally lifted. Facial massage is a great way to stimulate muscles, improve the circulation and get skin glowing. 'It's just the discipline that lets people down,' Su-Man says, pointedly. 'Treat your skincare routine like a ritual, not a chore. No shortcuts!' Check out Su-Man's list of helpful instructions. (see overleaf).

MAKE-UP – LESS IS MORE, AT LAST!

I'm lucky to have inherited my mum's good skin and, like Mum, I've never really worn much make-up. In fact, the only make-up I've ever seen my mum wearing is a pink Avon lipstick; I think she's had the same one for years, it's probably older than I am.

When I became fashion editor on a glossy women's magazine, I gradually started taking things a bit more seriously. The beauty director told me quite bluntly that no make-up make-up did, in fact, require effort and, like a luxury cosmetics pimp, started pushing free samples in my

direction. But even then, I didn't become a complete beauty junkie, and this newfound habit was easy to kick when I left to go freelance and realised that I couldn't actually afford to buy most of the products anyway.

These days, I still prefer the natural look; not-much-make-up make-up. And I'm delighted to find that as we get older, it's better to lay off the slap. As I've been taking this approach all my life, I feel like now I'm in my 50s, I've finally found the right decade. 'You can't pile on loads of shit. It ages you and can look a bit mutton!'exclaims make-up artist Ruby Hammer. This less-is-more era is endorsed by fellow make-up artist Sara Raeburn too: 'When you think of all the women whose looks you admire; like Inès de la Fressange, Sharon Stone or Nancy Shevell, none of them look as though they wear very much make-up, but they are all incredibly polished.' Well, that's a relief. Speaking to grown-up beauty experts Ruby and Sara, I am struck by the one constant that both women keep coming back to and that's taking time for you, doing what makes you feel good. I know from my own experience struggling with the work-life-blogging balance that it's quite easy to let things slide, to spend more time online than on yourself. Which is probably why everyone I speak to these days has taken up mindfulness …

There isn't one particular make-up formula; we all have different faces, different complexions and different personalities, so there are a few quick pointers on pages 82–3.

SU-MAN'S DIY MASSAGE ROUTINE

Follow this sequence after cleansing your face. All the exercises are easier to do sitting down.

(See a video of Su-Man online at www.su-man.com)

With elbows resting on a table, massage the face with moisturiser. Using the heels of both palms, start from the chin, moving along the jawbone up to the base of the ear 36 times (in Chinese culture the number six is considered a lucky number).

Take the heels of both your hands from the edge of your nostrils and press along in one continuous line underneath the cheekbones up to the edge of your ears. Always in one direction; never press downwards. You want to lift the face muscles upwards.

Take the middle fingers of both hands and press the area between your eyes and nose, at the very top of your nose. Press gently but firmly downwards following the nose line to the side of your nostrils. This also clears the sinuses and helps to improve your breathing.

4

Make two small claws with your four fingers of each hand. Put them together on the middle of your forehead and press quite firmly (without pulling the skin) in an outward direction, smoothly, to the temples.

5

Tap around the eye sockets with your fingertips, use the natural weight of the fingers. Do not tap too hard! Six times above and below the eye socket. Do not tap the eyelids. They are delicate and this can damage the eyes. This exercise reduces any puffiness or swelling above or below the eyes. Once a day is enough.

6

Finally, take the fingertips of both hands, and tap everywhere on the scalp and cranium quite strongly (using the natural weight of your fingers). When you have finished this sequence, drink a glass of warm water to help the chi flow. Always exfoliate and use a face mask once a week.

HOW TO ACHIEVE SIMPLE, AGELESS BEAUTY

1

DO THE RESEARCH

'Freedom comes from having a more effective regime,' advises Ruby Hammer. 'It doesn't need to take an hour – but it will take at least an hour's research. You need to make a concerted effort: try different blushers, find the best mascara, book in at the Bobbi Brown counter – go somewhere friendly where you can experiment. If you are stuck in a rut or not sure how to adapt your make-up, speak to the experts, but have an idea what you want. You have a good idea of what you want to achieve, so tell them, "This is how I used to look but this bit of me has faded, how do I reinforce it?" Working together with a make-up artist will give the best results. It's good to get expert advice – but don't let anybody bulldoze you!'

2

CONCEALER IS YOUR BIGGEST FRIEND

'You'll need two different concealers; one for under the eye and one to retouch the face and cover any age spots,' advises Sara. 'One of the main mistakes people make is using a concealer that's too light and you get that reverse panda eye effect. As you get older, you get darker under the eyes, so you need to adapt.' But go easy, warns Ruby: 'You need concealer to make your skin look uniform, but you don't want to look like you're wearing a mask. One of my favourites is Laura Mercier's Secret Camouflage Concealer; there are two different shades in the palette that you can customise till you get the right colour – then apply with a brush and gently pat into place.'

3

IT'S ALL ABOUT THE EYES

'Eyebrows are vitally important,' says Sara, 'As we mature, our eyebrows fade and often shed hair. I know it's a cliché, but they do frame your face, so make sure they are properly shaped and groomed – if you don't know what to do, get someone to do it for you. Learn how to draw them in with a brow pencil or powder. Gently stroke in fine feathery strokes from the inner eyebrow outwards and increase the amount where required (for gaps and missing hairs). Use a clean eyebrow brush or mascara brush and brush upwards to blend the colour. Practice makes perfect!' Keeping it simple is key, recommends Ruby: 'Curl your eyelashes and find a really good black or brown mascara. One that makes lashes look long and sexy; I love Max Factor Masterpiece and Benefit's They're Real! You only need one good coat for the day, but take your time applying it. Use a good neutral primer, then a woosh of shadow over the lids and add some definition with a dark eyeliner pencil (Benefit's They're Real! Push-Up Liner is great) or shadow around the eyelashes, as close to the eye line as possible.'

4

GET CHEEKY

'A flash of colour will make you look bright-eyed and bushy-tailed,' says Ruby, 'I like Yves Saint Laurent's Baby Doll Kiss & Blush or Bobbi Brown's Pot Rouge. As we age, the face does drop so smile and blend a cream blusher upwards and outwards; follow the curve of your cheekbone and look in the mirror to check that it's blended.'

6

LESS REALLY IS MORE

'Unless, of course, you're Joan Collins,' laughs Sara. 'There's no need to buy loads of products; they'll soon be out of date anyway. Fashion changes every five minutes, but if you want fashion, buy a new nail polish. It's about how you spend your money; buying less but finding the key products that really suit you – and then learning to use them. And if you use fewer products, you can spend more time doing your make-up!'

5

KISS OFF

'Avoid the ultra-matt effect,' advises Ruby. 'That is drying and can be quite ageing. I always use a lip balm first, pat off the excess and then apply the lippy; Clinique's Chubby Sticks are brilliant or try Benefit's Benebalm Hydrated Tinted Lip Balm. Lips get skinnier with age, so I use a neutral lip liner (matched to the natural lip tone) on top – Lipstick Queen Invisible Liner is genius – the liner slides over the balm and you can cheat it and make lips look bigger and more defined. If the liner's neutral, it will look natural.'

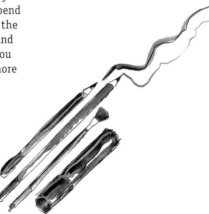

A growing number of selfless hairdressers are persuading their clients to relinquish the dye job and go grey. Unafraid of doing themselves out of work, they're thinking about what's good for the customer, not the cash register. 'I've always said I don't work in a way that makes people younger, I work in a way that makes them look the best they possibly can for their age,' international hair colourist Josh Wood (the man who created Kristen McMenamy's fabulous locks) tells me. 'And some people look better nearly natural.' Barnsley-born Wood agrees that there has been a slight turn of events when it comes to colouring, 'I do think that hair has to look hyper natural, otherwise it ages you more than if you don't colour it. And if you're becoming a slave to your roots, then your hair's the wrong colour.'

'Beauty begins the moment you decide to be yourself.'

— Coco Chanel

Beauty journalist and yoga teacher Catherine Turner agrees, 'I was going to the hairdressers every few weeks to have my roots done, and in the end it was such a relief to go natural.' At the time, Catherine was the blonde-haired beauty director of a glossy magazine, with a secret plan to go freelance, do more yoga and embark on a life-changing trip to an ashram in India. 'I didn't want to be one of those high-maintenance women, all blonde highlights and Botox. I knew I was going to change my life and felt that my exterior didn't match my interior. My hair felt less authentic.' Founder of White Hot Hair, a range of luxury products for grey hair, Jayne Mayled had a similar experience, 'I wanted something that reflected the way I felt. I went grey early on and kept dyeing it but it became harder and harder to do and not look like Paul McCartney.'

Wood insists that the greying process is about changing the hair colour, not growing it out, 'It's not about letting go; it's about accepting more grey but it has to be the right amount, the right tone and the right overall feel.' Of course, hair colour is closely linked to personal style, make-up and the overall image and so making this significant change might require a slight shift in the wardrobe department, too. Be careful with beige, the wrong tone might just kill your complexion, and add some stronger, brighter colours. No need to go for the crazy, full-on 'look at me, I work in textiles' vibe; think head of the International Monetary Fund Christine Lagarde looking the business in a pink Chanel jacket and pearl earrings or a gorgeous silk scarf, worn over a simple black outfit. Try more tonal bluey greys and charcoals; navy and aubergine always look chic and the good news is that black becomes an option again, though personally I prefer head-to-toe navy.

'Grey has to be a statement, it's got to look striking,' points out Josh. 'Never middle-of-the-road. I think you can either turn up the volume 100 per cent and wear brighter lipstick and so on, or go in the other direction for that incredibly natural Scandi-look.'

There's definitely a growing community of women who believe that looking and feeling good doesn't involve trying to look younger, but we still have further to go. I'm astounded when Josh tells me that some of his clients have their roots done every 10 days. 'It's not the obvious ones, I'm talking about women in high-powered positions who are judged by their peers.' Not all women have the option of going grey; there are areas of business and industry where ageism is still rife. Hello BBC!

A situation where we have to remain forever young to be credible and to do so have to keep up ridiculous beauty regimes is not a healthy state of affairs. 'We need to see more positive images of older women,' says Jayne Mayled. 'There's still a huge inequality. When a man goes grey, he's viewed as a silver fox, when a woman does it, she's a granny. It's very subliminal, but I am treated with more delicacy by taxi drivers – and definitely let out at traffic junctions more.'

Now a fully qualified yoga teacher, Catherine admits that in spite of all the compliments, going grey isn't an easy ride, 'I get stopped in the street by people who tell me that they like my grey hair but even so, sometimes in my head, I still feel old.

It's weird when I see a picture of myself.' Ditching the hair dye requires a certain level of confidence and self-acceptance, as Catherine agrees, 'The hair thing is definitely me coming to terms with getting older, I know in my heart that I can't go back.'

GOING *AU NATURALE*

If you want to go *au naturale*, here's what to do according to Josh Wood:

1. Get some good advice. You need to be psychologically ready and you need to find the right hairdresser. You're going to have a one year to 18 months' deep relationship with your hairdresser, so make sure you're happy with them. Consider colour and suitability. Think about the percentage of

grey you are and what you want/can live with. If you're a brunette, the transition is not going to be easy, but no pain no gain. There will be a period, six to nine months, in when you'll get that 'Duracell battery' look (large roots and different coloured ends); that's the moment when you realise that you might have to go a bit shorter.

2. Maintenance: there are lots of things to do to keep the hair hydrated and soft, grey hair looks and feels dryer. Treatments, glazes, glosses, toners, the correct shampoo and conditioner. You have to keep grey hair looking supple and shiny like Christine Lagarde's. Her short, sharp chic bob looks healthy and glossy; there's

a lot of work involved but it's worth it. If she was looking to move into Number 10 (Downing Street), we'd all be voting for her.

CATHERINE TURNER'S PICK OF THE BEST GREY HAIR PRODUCTS

According to Catherine Turner, her scalp is much healthier since growing out her colour, and her hair is less high-maintenance. Here are Catherine's favourite grey hair products:

Bumble and Bumble Surf Foam Wash Creme Rinse
Gently cleans and conditions, leaving hair with a little 'guts'.

Purely Perfect Cleansing Creme
The equivalent of no-foam cleanser, this lotion shampoo and conditioner-in-one is full of botanicals and leaves my hair squeaky clean and shiny as a child's. Takes a bit of getting used to as there are no suds. It's super-fast because there's no need for conditioner.

Pureology Perfect 4 Platinum Miracle Filler Treatment
This finishing product is great for taking away the brassiness and bringing the sparkle back to blondes – but a little goes a long, long way. I've found some blue/lavender hair products can leave a tell-tale tinge on white hair but this treatment is quite subtle.

Aveda Pure Abundance Style Prep
I comb a little of this through towel-dried hair after washing to add just a little oomph.

Aveda Damage Remedy Restructuring Conditioner

This is the protein treatment I use when my hair starts to snap and break – it's a real fix-it treatment and good to use every now and again.

Sans [Ceuticals] Volumising Hair Wash and Hydratant

These are from a great chemical-free beauty range from New Zealand. They're creamy (and I don't normally like that in a shampoo) but feel super-light on the hair, have a subtle smell and leave hair feeling like new.

John Frieda Luxurious Volume Touchably Full Shampoo and Conditioner

I think this is the best high-street buy for fine hair – and once again has just the right balance of cleanness and condition.

NON-GREY MATTERS

I was going to say that with hair, as with make-up, it's best to take the natural approach and then I remembered fabulous flame-haired, 74-year-old Grace Coddington. Don't forget her partner is a hairdresser, though. So, if you want to carry on colouring, find yourself a bloody good hairdresser and usher in the blusher.

Alternatively, avoid the Macca look by keeping hair as close to your own colour as possible. As a general rule: lighter and brighter complements the complexion and darker can be harsher.

'The cut is everything,' says Guy Healey, my own personal hairdresser .

'It's important because it sets you apart and a simple, natural-looking hairstyle looks good whatever your age. I'd recommend a miniscule trim on a regular basis – I always feel loads better when I've had a trim and I've hardly got any hair left on my head!'

'Use a conditioning treatment once a week,' advises Josh Wood. 'It's important to keep hair in a decent condition, especially if it's thinning.'

Don't overdo the styling: a regular blow-dry is fine but a great big do can backfire. For a friend's 50th birthday party, I decided to have a go at the elegant, 1960s-style chignon I used to wear in my 20s. It was a lot trickier to manage than when I last tried it, but I had more patience then and a lot less grey hair. I ended up washing it out; it was that or go to the party looking like I was wearing a powdered wig.

And that's probably where the moral of the story lies; dress to suit who you are now, not who you were.

'You can get older and still be rock 'n' roll.'

– Kristen McMenamy

SCENT SENSE
BY VICCI BENTLEY

I asked my friend, perfume expert and award-winning writer Vicci Bentley to make some scent sense:

'A great scent can work like a "legal high" to pick you up on down days or give you the chutzpah to face a room of strangers. As the invisible accessory that defines your style, perfume has a near-magical ability to pull a look together – or not. For there comes a time when that "in your face" hyper-pungent gourmand number with the half-life of strontium (yes, I'm thinking Angel) becomes the olfactory equivalent of mutton dressed as lamb. Ditto sweet fruity florals which really are olfactory alcopops. If you're hearing "lush pear", "crisp, juicy apple" or, heaven forefend, "candyfloss" back away from that counter, now.

'Thinking women's scents tend to be softer and less obvious, but with a warmth and sillage (the intriguing, but not overpowering trail you leave behind

when you leave the room) that becomes your personal signature. Among the most sensual are the chypres, so-called after the French for Cyprus, where the suave oak moss that characterises them originally came from. Great classics such as Miss Dior (far too grown up to sound like a teen scent!), Femme by Rochas and Eau d'Hermès all come from this fragrance family – and if you've loved them for years, why change? Whereas girls are fragrance flirts, market research tells us that once we're past 30, we're increasingly likely to commit to a single, "signature" scent with each decade. By the time we're 65, we've probably worn "the one" for the past 20 years.

'Can a scent date you? Thanks to on-going advances in scent technology, modern sprays tend to be longer-lasting than those launched a couple of decades ago. On the downside, since many traditional ingredients are now either restricted or banned, classic scents which once contained them have been "edited" – one reason why you suspect

your old favourite doesn't smell as deep and dirty as it used to.

'But don't turn your nose up at new versions of classics such as Eau Première, the youthfully "lite" version of grand old lady Chanel No5, which many people of all ages find fresher and easier to wear than the original. Or maybe you fancy something completely different? In the same way your style refines in your 30s and 40s, it's not unknown to go off a type of scent post-menopause. Blame it on dwindling hormones but, to my utter surprise, I'm becoming less leathery and more floral. Intense "cleavage heavers" do seem a bit off-message these days.

'That doesn't mean I'm all lace and lavender, though. My fixes are "get up and go" mood-boosters laced with citrus and orange blossom, possibly scent's most euphoric ingredients. Japanese studies suggest grapefruit (as in Jo Malone's Grapefruit Cologne) can even help you to appear slimmer and younger! My current "self-medication" is Eau de Magnolia by Editions de Parfums Frederic Malle – a creamy, lemony magnolia on a reassuring mossy base.

'One last caution: try not to overspray. Our sense of smell dulls progressively with age, so sousing yourself in scent could prove a dead 'old girl' giveaway. If your skin's dry, scent evaporates faster, so a perfumed body cream may help to preserve your aura. Above all, don't be the ditzy crone people shuffle away from on the bus. Those around you can catch your scent even if you've lost the drift. Now, where did I put that bottle …'

WHAT I'VE LEARNT ABOUT BEAUTY

1

TAKE A BIT MORE TIME GETTING READY

Throwing make-up on and immediately looking fabulous is inversely proportionate to age. Easy enough when you're a dewy-skinned teenager, less likely when you're closer to retirement than graduation. And a last-minute rush is never a good way to start the day.

2

LESS IS MORE

No need for too much of anything, it just ends up looking caked on and Barbara Cartland-ish. Au naturel, no-make-up make-up works best.

3

KEEP MOVING

Go for a walk, do pilates.

4

IT'S WORTH PAYING FOR A DECENT HAIRCUT

The thing with hair is not to look too neat, or too set. All those fabulous French fashion editors look a little undone – but remember, there's a fine line between fashionably dishevelled and Care in the Community.

5

GREY IS GOOD

(see page 80) – when it is properly looked after.

6

CLEANSING IS IMPORTANT AS YOU GET OLDER

Pores enlarge and dirt and make-up get caught in the cracks. Which is why I use Clinique's Sonic Cleansing Brush.

7

GET BROWS SHAPED AND TINTED BY A PROFESSIONAL

Ditto moustache-threading and pedicures.

8

BUY A MAGNIFYING MIRROR BUT DON'T LOOK IN IT TOO OFTEN

9

SO MANY INGREDIENTS, SO LITTLE SKIN

Look out for products with: Antioxidants (cell protection) Hyaluronic acid (line plumping and firming) Retinol (Vit A; firming).

10

AND IF ALL ELSE FAILS

dim the switches …

Kay Montano

OVER THE LAST 30 YEARS, THE LONDON-BORN MAKE-UP ARTIST HAS WORKED WITH ALL THE BIGGEST AND BEST MAGAZINES, PHOTOGRAPHERS AND MODELS IN THE WORLD. TOGETHER WITH THE ACTRESS THANDIE NEWTON, SHE IS THE CO-AUTHOR OF THE BEAUTY AND LIFESTYLE WEBSITE *THANDIEKAY*.

'What would I say to my 15-year-old self? My 15-year-old self wouldn't have listened!'

ON AGE

A woman reaches her peak around the exact same time that society and the media say she's no longer relevant. It's a strange conundrum. My favourite term is, 'Age is not an aberration'. We are meant to get old. Accepting this has been an epiphany, for me. It's great to finally feel liberated – and I don't give a shit about not being cat-called.

ON BEING A MAKE-UP ARTIST

It's like having a magic wand. It's selling a dream. It takes a lot of talent – amazing photographers and stylists – to create an iconic photograph. I see my job as preaching to the unconverted. I'm attracting them by saying: 'Isn't this gorgeous and cool?' Or, 'Why don't we have a black model, an older model?' Change will come from the inside. I want to change things, be the Trojan horse. Be a maverick like Diana Vreeland.

ON CELEBRITY

We live in a society where a girl's worth is her sexuality, where Kim Kardashian is famous for making a sex tape. The most influential woman in the world is famous for making a sex tape! It's very regressive. I don't have a TV and I don't have fashion magazines in my house. They're full of false promises and illusions. I'd rather do something creative and not be dictated to. But I'm not some worthy killjoy – I do love a *Grey's Anatomy* boxset.

ON THE OLD LADY REVOLUTION

I think we have to be careful that this doesn't turn into a ghetto of naffness. We focus too much on the difference between people: black/white, old/young, when we should be looking at the similarities. Pressure to change has to come from within, from mavericks like Richard Avedon who refused to work with American *Harper's Bazaar* in the 70s when they rejected his model choice, China Machado.

ON RELAXING

I work out a lot. I've got a dog and a house that's never finished. If you want to do things that make you happy, you have to do them yourself. I really like creating things, working on creative projects. It's a lot of work, but Thandie and I do the website ourselves because it has to be representative. I'm a worrier by nature, totally neurotic. I'm like Woody Allen. I constantly distract myself from this feeling by being creative. By doing something beautiful with my life.

ON BEAUTY

Some women are beautiful all their lives. Others bloom at different times. I can't stand it when people say, 'Oh don't you look good for your age.' This is what

47 looks like. It's best not to define yourself by your looks, it's about who you are as a human being.

Sue Kreitzman

ARTIST, CURATOR AND ONE OF THE STARS OF THE CHANNEL 4 DOCUMENTARY *FABULOUS FASHIONISTAS*, SUE KREITZMAN IS A FORMER FOOD WRITER AND TV COOK, AN EXPATRIATE NEW YORKER LIVING IN LONDON.

'I didn't realise I was old until I watched the documentary Fabulous Fashionistas.'

ON THE OLD LADY REVOLUTION

We're intelligent women and we're having an impact, making a difference and that's what it should be about. Not just walking around looking pretty. People pay attention to older women now; we're here, we're not going to disappear, get used to it.

ON ART

I was a food writer and TV cook for many years. I still don't know what happened, I had some sort of psychotic breakdown and became completely obsessed with drawing. I was working day and night with marker pens and nail varnish, drawing like crazy. I had to keep the windows open because of the fumes. I was high on art, that's for sure. My world is like a very weird Disneyland for grown-ups, I'm in a constant state of art arousal.

ON SUE KREITZMAN STYLE

My red glasses cost £6 from London's Spitalfields Market. The guy who sells them has adopted me – I think he usually charges £15. My clothes are custom-made for me; I collect fabrics from all over the world and the artist Lauren Shanley turns these into collages for my wrap coats, and Diane Goldie hand-paints jackets and kimonos for me. My accessories are pure colour, pure imagination and rather mad. I make a lot of them myself. I make art, I curate art and I wear art. I feel good when I'm wrapped in art.

ON AGE

I've never really grown up; the way I work, the way I see, the way I dress ... keeps me young, keeps me free. You get a little more decrepit: my hearing and eyesight are not what they used to be and

I get tired. I'm 75 so I take naps, I can't put in the excessive hours any more but I'm still prolific. As long as you've still got your marbles and can put one foot in front of the other, getting old is an adventure and a privilege. Enjoy the hell out of it.

ON BEING A STYLE ICON

I never liked fashion. I've always done my own thing. Living in New York in the 1970s, I used to wear a lot of vintage, a lot of ethnic jewellery. I've always been quite flamboyant. When I worked on a cookery magazine, one of my colleagues said to me, 'I can't wait for you to come into work every day to see what you're wearing.' And now I've been on the cover of the *Sunday Times Style* magazine. Holy Moly, it took me 70-odd-years to be one of the cool girls.

ON WHAT YOU'D SAY TO YOUR 15-YEAR-OLD SELF

I'd say, 'You're not going to believe what's going to happen.' And my 15-year-old self would say, 'I'm having a very strange hallucination.'

Wendy Dagworthy

ONE OF THE MOST INFLUENTIAL WOMEN IN BRITISH FASHION, AND ONE OF THE FOUNDERS OF LONDON FASHION WEEK, THE FORMER DESIGNER AND ACADEMIC RETIRED FROM THE ROYAL COLLEGE OF ART AFTER 16 YEARS LAST SUMMER. SHE REMAINS ON THE BOARD OF THE BRITISH FASHION COUNCIL.

'I can't wait to spend time doing all the things I can't do while I'm at work like travelling around India for six months, going horse-racing and renovating our new home.'

ON BEING A FASHION DESIGNER

It was so much fun being a designer in the 80s, everything was new and not stylized at all. You just threw a show together. It was amazing seeing my clothes in the shops, and people wearing them – not always as intended. Today it's much more cut-throat and very corporate. Fashion is totally global – but each brand has its own identity and this is something I advise young designers to do; to have their own identity and have faith in themselves.

ON AGE

I don't mind getting older. I don't think about age. I believe in making the most of your life, you never know what's going to happen. When I closed my fashion company, I didn't keep harking back to the good old days. I moved on to the next stage of my life. You've got to be positive otherwise life will be a misery.

ON ART SCHOOL

I'm very lucky to have taught at the two best fashion colleges in London, to achieve great things with great students. It was a fantastic honour to become Dean at the Royal College of Art: seeing students progress, meeting amazing people, running things. Central Saint Martins in the 1990s was a really exciting time too. We had such great students, like Hussein Chalayan, Stella McCartney and Alexander McQueen. I love seeing students develop, work and progress; it's so much harder today with tuition fees and stuff, but I do think graduates are much more professional, braver and more carefree in spirit. The world has opened up and they don't blink an eyelid about moving to another continent or city.

ON STYLE

I never understand it when people say they can't find anything suitable for their age. Why do you have to have something different? I dress like the students. I live in simple tunic dresses from Cos (lots of my ex-students work there), always add a big necklace and my signature silver bangles (I counted 20 jangling on one arm on the day of our interview). My husband John buys them for me from antique markets, for birthdays, Christmas and anniversaries. I've been wearing a stripy Saint James' matelot and Levi's 501s for years, and I'll be wearing them even more now I've retired.

ON GOING GREY

I'd been dyeing my hair red for years but it had started to look a bit dated, a bit 1970s. So I thought, get rid. It was a huge step and it took three years and a lot of perseverance – there were times when I just I wanted to go to the hairdressers and get it dyed back again. You have to have a lot of confidence in yourself, to tell yourself , 'I am going to look older.' But I

think as you grow older, your complexion changes and grey hair does suit your face, it doesn't look as harsh as dyed hair. I love not having to worry about going to the hairdressers.

ON WHAT YOU'D SAY TO YOUR 15-YEAR-OLD SELF

Enjoy yourself. Believe in yourself. Be nice, be positive, don't look back in regret, follow your dreams but always leave something to chance.

THE WARDROBE GLUE

Confidence comes from finding clothes and accessories that work in real life. Not just on catwalks, in glossy magazines or 'today i'm wearing' blog posts. These reliable, figure-flattering essentials are what I like to call Wardobe Glue. One of the reasons I rarely post photographs of myself on *That's Not My Age* is because I wear the same clothes, a lot. Not in a skanky, 'I've given up' kind of way; this is my grown-up, fuss-free uniform. The one fashion rule I do agree with is to buy multiples of the basics; the stuff you'll wear to death. If our younger years are all about experimenting and identity-finding, *Generation FAB* is all about streamlining and refining. Over the years we've figured out what suits and what doesn't – now is the time to exploit this personal style knowledge to the max.

Style is a resilient Catherine Deneuve to fashion's flash-in-the-pan, famous-for five-minutes reality TV star. Fashion trends don't matter. What is important is wearing what you like, what makes you happy. Sometimes this involves re-visiting stuff we've loved before, and now have the confidence to love again. I'm thinking; the khaki military jacket, Levi's 501s and the jumpsuit. Choosing confidence-boosting clothes that fit, flatter and feel comfortable is the basis for effortless style. And I know comfort factor doesn't sound like a glamorous proposition, but no one ever looked confident hobbling down the street in stupid four-inch heels. Why else do you think Deneuve has spent the best part of her life wearing an Yves Saint Laurent tuxedo?

Finding the perfect Wardrobe Glue may take effort but you're going to be old for a very long time, so it's worth putting in the groundwork. Once the essentials are in place, the uniform perfected, add a final flourish and you're ready for action.

MY STYLE BASICS

1. SHOES THAT YOU CAN ACTUALLY WALK IN

There's a photograph of Coco Chanel reclining on the beach in Biarritz in 1920 that, to me, signifies the birth of Casual Glamour. White sun hat pulled on over neatly bobbed hair, oversized men's cardigan over a simple white shirt, legs crossed under a knitted jersey below-the-knee skirt and – the highlight of this chic-as-you-like outfit – leather co-respondent shoes on her feet. Chanel is wearing men's shoes, flat shoes that she can walk in. As well as the early stages of the garçonne look, this photograph signifies a time when, after the First World War, women were becoming increasingly independent. The canny designer may not have been

the first woman to wear men's shoes – I'm sure the Land Army, the suffragettes and other women who weren't reclining on the beaches beat her to it – but wearing her own designs, epitomizing her fashion brand and hanging out with glamorous people (sound familiar?) generated loads of press coverage and was key to her success. Focusing on comfort, ease of movement and simplicity, Chanel created outfits to suit a more active lifestyle – a sporty, modern, wearable look. As Diana Vreeland once said, 'She invented the 20th century for women.' And she wore comfortable shoes.

For the majority of my life I've worn comfy shoes, too; I'm more than happy when the brogue is in vogue – which is very much the case as I type these words. Fashion is all 'boyfriend this' and 'boyfriend that'; the elegant tomboy style of designers like Céline's Phoebe Philo and J. Crew's Jenna Lyons. Images of women constantly in the paparazzi's glare like Sofia Coppola and Alexa Chung have trickled into the mainstream and flooded the internet. Fortunately, this modern-day Gentlewoman Style – a slightly oversized shirt with slim pants and run-around shoes – is infinitely wearable. Even when your significant other is more of an old boy than boyfriend.

Of course there have been times when I've hobbled off sensible shoe street: as a teenager I'd cram my feet into secondhand 1960s winkle pickers to go clubbing at the Calypso Bar on Blackpool Pleasure Beach – all plastic palm trees, bad hair and the occasional lost coach party looking for Cannon & Ball. And then there was

the fashion editor phase, when I flounced around magazine land in pointy kitten heels and clothes from my extended wardrobe: the fashion cupboard. It was great to embark on a freelance career and feel completely unencumbered. Out came the Converse All Stars; I hadn't worn Chucks since my 20s so, in a youth-obsessed industry, this was probably a subliminal attempt to be down with the kids. But, after a few months, my feet started to hurt. I was 40, freelance and feeling the pain.

> 'If a woman rebels against high heeled shoes, she should take care to do it in a very smart hat.'
>
> – George Bernard Shaw

Wearing flimsy flat shoes for extended periods of time, or just being over 40, can trigger a painful condition called plantar fasciitis (when a band of tissue in the foot called the plantar fascia becomes damaged or thickens). I'm not sure if I actually had this, I just read about it in the newspaper. Self-diagnosis is a wonderful thing. What I am convinced about though, is that there's going to be a plantar fasciitis epidemic when all those young, Generation Y women who've spent their 20s shuffling around in horrible Ugg boots and plimsolls with paper-thin soles hit mid-life. After

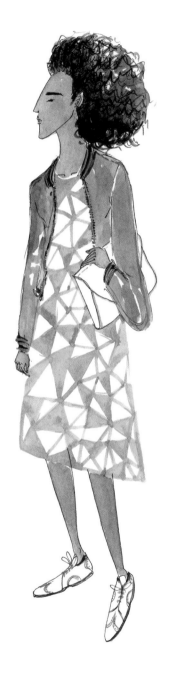

THE TEN BEST SHOE STYLES

1

CHELSEA BOOTS
Look Mod-tastic with
black cigarette pants and
a roll-neck sweater.

2

BROGUES
Go with trousers, skirts,
dresses, everything. Just
add colourful opaques
when unleashing the legs.

3

**DECORATIVE LEATHER
PUMPS (FLAT OR WITH A
LOW HEEL)**
Good with jeans, perfect
with an evening maxi skirt
and a silk blouse or T-shirt.

4

RIDING BOOTS
Christine Lagarde,
that's all.

5

LOAFERS
Best worn with rolled-up
jeans or chinos and a flash
of ankle.

6

**LOW- TO MID-HEELED
LEATHER ANKLE BOOTS**
Embrace French *Vogue*
editor-style with slim leg
jeans and a kick-ass jacket.

7

BIRKENSTOCKS
May they be in
fashion forever.

8

**LOW-RISE PLATFORM
SANDALS OR CLOGS**
Just Scandi-licious with
a tunic dress and
colourful tights.

9

KITTEN HEEL COURT
Keep it chic with an
elegant dress.

10

METALLIC SLINGBACKS
The stylish way to swing
your Capri pants.

visiting numerous osteopaths and physiotherapists, various diagnoses and treatments, I eventually ended up wearing orthotics: big plastic insoles that do not fit inside any attractive, normal-sized shoes. I lived with them for a couple of years and can still remember being on a commercial shoot with my clearly visible, oversized orthotics wedged into a pair of cheap canvas ballet pumps, feeling awkward and ancient next to all the bright young things from the ad agency. It was there and then that I decided that rather than waste hundreds of pounds on hideous orthopaedic supports, I'd spend the money on decent shoes instead. Sensible sturdy shoes from Church's, Margaret Howell and Grenson. And my feet have been happy ever since. So, I'm sure I don't need to over-emphasise the importance of a comfy shoe – we all know it's impossible to be FABulous when your feet hurt.

2. THE LOVELY BLUE SHIRT

Some people swear by the classic white but I much prefer the Lovely Blue Shirt (LBS). A garment whose value I appreciated early on in life; having left the Girl Guides after a week (it just wasn't as good as the Brownies), I swiftly realised that I needed to make use of the brand-new uniform my mum had spent all her money on. I was a big Bay City Rollers fan. A tartan kilt was chopped up, plaid trim stitched around the collar and cuffs, ERIC attached in big wonky letters across the back of the not-so-lovely blue polyester shirt. But this outward display of fandom was short-lived;

ridiculed by older boys on the top deck of the bus I learnt a very quick lesson about embellishment, DIY and musical tastes. Keep it simple, keep it real (cotton or linen) and keep it to yourself.

Guaranteed to look cool throughout a heat wave or a hot flush, the LBS goes with everything: pencil skirts, maxi skirts, most trouser styles, and adds instant chic appeal. As well as offering excellent arm coverage (should you want it), its complexion-enhancing properties are second to none. And, that's quite a lot of boxes ticked. One of my favourite blue shirt fashion moments is an old image of Grace Kelly (from the Howell Conant book) looking just as perfect in a button-down LBS and mannish pleated trousers, as when decked out in her trademark heroine style. See also the fabulous Rosella Jardini – there's a brilliant picture of the 62-year-old Italian fashion consultant taken by French photographer Garance Doré. One glance is all it takes to appreciate the wonder of the LBS. My advice is to keep things relaxed and opt for a slightly oversized, borrowed-from-the-boys style.

Of course, the essential denim shirt falls into this category too. Worn by cowboys, rebels, rock stars and fashion VIPs from Clint Eastwood to Kate Moss, James Dean to Jane Birkin, this hard-working garment combines counter-cultural style and catwalk credentials. Whether it's on the catwalk or not, this fail-safe fabric is always in my wardrobe. Denim is timeless, functional and durable – the essential shirt is the perfect year-round staple.

SHIRTS:

- The denim shirt can and should be worn doubled-up with jeans. Avoid the Texan tuxedo-look by wearing different shades. Try a faded shirt with dark-blue jeans, or deep indigo shirt and black jeans.

- For everyday glamour, slip on a denim shirt with a leather pencil skirt or pair of black cigarette pants.

- Deeper shades of blue have a smarter edge and are acceptable in the office.

3. TIME-SAVING BLACK TROUSERS

Women haven't always worn trousers. Bifurcated garments (along with the leg-o-mutton sleeve, bifurcated is up there on my list of top-notch fashion terms) appeared in the early 20th century, as practical attire for cycling in. By the 1930s, Hollywood movie stars like Katharine Hepburn, Greta Garbo and Marlene Dietrich had embraced androgynous style and were striding around on set in tailored black trousers. But it wasn't until Yves Saint Laurent introduced Le Smoking in the 70s – and on the other side of the Atlantic, Halston launched 'one-stop dressing' – that trousers began to seep into modern life. Though not the workplace; even the 80s power suit came with a just-above-the knee pencil skirt I can't even remember the last time I wore a skirt, possibly not in this century. Why

bother when time-saving trousers always look chic and save on faffage? In fact, if it wasn't for a pair of Acne stretch canvas 'Skin' trousers (mid-rise, slim cigarette leg, zip-up the back) and the precious minutes they save, allowing me time to complete a blog post and chuck it into cyberspace as I gulp down my breakfast, this book probably wouldn't exist. So, until Google invent a *Wallace & Gromit*-type machine to dress me in the morning, I'll be calling upon such reliable wardrobe basics to help get me out of the door in 10 minutes flat.

Obviously, over time, silhouettes and shapes change. There's a pair of low-slung, Dirk Bikkembergs boot-cut needle cords that haven't seen daylight since the 90s and I'm itching to wear them again with a pair of pointy flats. Lifelong black trouser-wearer Patti Smith has gone from 70s flares – shown off beautifully with one leg cocked up on the mantelpiece in Robert Mapplethorpe's photograph – to drainpipes and back again, before finally settling on a slouchy pair of rolled-up Ann Demeulemeester trousers and bovver boots. Quality of fabric and investing in the perfect cut are the most important factors, as brand owner and fashion expert Kim Winser tells me: 'So many [trousers] are badly designed and cut, made in cheap fabrics that certainly do not flatter. Black trousers are an important investment – they're easy for work, evenings or just to run around every day – the right pair will do you proud time and time again.'

Last winter, I lived in Eileen Fisher's waxed skinny jeans. I'm all for that leg-enhancing, fabulous femme combination of black cigarette pants and leather ankle boots. Come summer, there's the relaxed option of jersey harem pants and a safari shirt, or the Jean Seberg meets Sofia Coppola Capri pant. I have an ancient pair of stretch Capri pants from Gap that I roll out every summer – they may not be Yves Saint Laurent, but they've done me proud; this kind of time-saving trouser is timeless too.

4. AN OUTSTANDING COAT

Visiting an exhibition by the Mexican artist Gabriel Kuri at our local South London Gallery, a couple of years ago, Mr *That's Not My Age* stopped to admire one of the sculptures. *Shelter* was an exploration of the 'imagery associated with housing, aid and economics', composed of various items lined up against the wall: including cut-up credit cards and an overladen coat rack. 'That looks like our hallway,' he said. Although the Blog Widower may disagree, I find it's best to have a good selection of outerwear: a Coat Wardrobe. Sometimes this outer layer is the only one people see, and who wants to wear the same thing all winter? Much better to mix it up – and there are so many fabulous styles to choose from: cocoon shapes, capes and blanket coats, trenches, Crombies, parkas, military jackets. And there's really no need to abuse the credit card, a decent Coat Wardrobe can be found on the high street; most of my coats are from Brixton Market.

Look around at the bus stop in mid-January, I can guarantee there'll be a crowd of people looking pasty in big, black coats. I recommend going for a fabulous, stand-out-from-the-crowd number.

At my age, death-warmed-up is not a good option and so it's better to consider something, well, a little livelier. Here are my suggestions:

THE VINTAGE STYLE

Miuccia Prada loves to experiment with fabrics; the influential designer has said, 'I make ugly clothes from ugly materials: simply bad taste. But they end up looking good anyway.' Which is why there's always an eye-catching coat in a vintage-inspired pattern in Prada's ready-to-wear collection. My all-time favourite coat is a vintage 1960s faux fur leopard-print number, bought in a junk shop years ago and nicknamed The Beast. I'm not quite sure when fake fur became faux – probably around the time Anna Wintour was slapped in the face with a tofu pie – but let's go with contemporary fashion terminology here. The Beast has accompanied me all over the world: Paris, New York and the Arctic Circle (with a down gilet and thermals underneath) but, sadly, the only place I can't wear it is London Fashion Week. The fear of being pestered by young street style bloggers looking for older material is too great. A leopard-print coat is like catnip to that bunch. Big Catnip. I know, I know – every shop on the high street has a cheap animal-print Kate-Moss-a-like cover-up these days, but The Beast is a superior animal. Fortunately, I'm also the proud owner of The Bear, a 1950s fuzzy brown coat that provides a cosy, low-key alternative for skulking around in.

THE RELIABLE CLASSIC

To the anti-beige brigade this may not sound like much of a statement, but some days a more business-like approach is required. And a sharp, single-breasted coat in charcoal, navy or tweed says 'fuss-free and fabulously chic'.

The elegant camel wrap coat is another classic worth considering. Check out Veronica Lake in Preston Sturges' wonderful film *Sullivan's Travels* – the epitome of gorgeousness and glamour – and ignore Sue Kreitzman's 'beige will kill you'. It won't. Just bask in camel's golden glow and wear with leopard print and bright red. There's a reason why MaxMara has made millions from this timeless style.

THE BRILLIANT COVER-UP

At the age of 10, my mum bought me a garish sky-blue anorak. I sold it a couple of weeks later at an impromptu yard sale, for 50p. Fortunately, over the years, my opinion of cheerful cover-ups has changed. Now I can see the attraction, really I can. In autumn I bought a mustard coloured, collarless coat from Cos and it reminded me of a lovely 1953 American *Vogue* cover photographed by Erwin Blumenfeld; four images of the same model repeated against a black background. In each shot the model is wearing the same jacket but in a different colour: gold, airforce blue, rose pink and scarlet. And, just like the modern-day bus stop scenario, these brilliant colours really do stand out amidst the blackness.

> 'Fashion is what you're offered four times a year by designers. And style is what you choose.'
>
> – Lauren Hutton

5. EVERYDAY DENIM JEANS

The best thing about denim is that it gets better with age. And we all know how we feel about that phenomenon. To me, an old pair of jeans is like a brilliant comfort blanket – faded, soft, worn – one with not too many dribble stains that I can safely leave the house in.

Chloe Lonsdale, founder and creative director of MiH jeans, feels the same: 'That's what's so beautiful about denim, it's designed to last and live with you. Jeans get beaten and bashed and become part of your life.' Born into a denim dynasty, Chloe explains her love affair with the sturdy fabric: 'I'm not really a denim geek. For me it's more of a lifestyle, a denim way of dressing. The spirit of wearing jeans is not about glamour, more bare-faced chic. Denim adds a bit of attitude and energy without doing too much.' Exactly.

Fortunately, I've always had the kind of job where I can add a bit of daily denim attitude, apart from one with a mail order company in the late 80s where, early on in my fashion career, I was admonished

EIGHT PERFECT PAIRS OF JEANS

1

J. CREW'S TOOTHPICK (ANKLE-LENGTH) JEANS
My current favourites. Perfect with Chelsea boots in winter and Birkenstocks in summer.

2

J BRAND 8112
Features a skinny/straight leg, a nice mid-rise and comes highly recommended by a regular *That's Not My Age* follower.

3

GAP REAL STRAIGHT, MID-RISE JEANS.
I'm a massive fan of Gap jeans and own several pairs. This style is simple and straightforward with no logos or branding.

4

UNIQLO STRAIGHT SKINNY FIT
A decent cheap option. Only problem is, the dye doesn't appear to be fixed so I always end up with dark-blue hands and what looks like a five o'clock shadow. Don't invite me round to your house if you've got a white sofa.

5

APC JEAN ÉTROIT COURT
My best pair of jeans ever are over 20 years old and from APC. I've just bought this cropped leg, straight, low-rise style. Made from Japanese denim (with 2 per cent polyurethane) that feels a bit like cardboard for the first few wears.

6

MIH PHOEBE SLIM JEAN
A slimmer-legged boyfriend style that founder Chloe Lonsdale advises is 'easy to wear, has a great silhouette and is popular right now'.

7

NOT YOUR DAUGHTER'S JEANS
Dubious name, available in various leg shapes, these are 'comfortable and flattering and you never have a fat day', according to a reliable source.

8

LEVI'S 501S
The original and the best. For a more figure-hugging style, Levi's Curve ID has a good rep.

for looking like I'd 'grabbed my clothes out of the laundry basket'. When the boss ordered me to invest in a briefcase, I knew my days were numbered.

Denim hasn't always been an easy, everyday option. In the 1950s, when another kind of age barrier existed, teenagers rebelled by dressing differently to their parents, by adopting the clothes worn by rock 'n' roll heroes and movie stars, who in turn were wearing working-class gear to break with convention and challenge the social order. As well as bad boy rebels like James Dean and Marlon Brando, Marilyn Monroe famously wore jeans on and off set. On the set of 1954's *The River of No Return* and again in 1961's *The Misfits*, Eve Arnold, the first female Magnum photographer, beautifully captured Monroe in jeans, a white shirt, cowboy boots and a Lee Storm Rider denim jacket. The first female star in double denim? Could be.

Today's denim isn't all rough and rugged (unless you're a staunch fan of the Japanese selvedge variety). It's pre-shrunk, worn-and-torn, distressed, beaten, bleached and over-dyed, sometimes at great cost to the environment. But we have DuPont to thank for Lycra. In my younger days I was tough enough to handle the stiff, unwashed material but now it's all about comfort and ease and not performing the Heimlich Manoeuvre on myself every time I sit down. I once saw the 56-year-old dancer/theatre artist Wendy Houston in a short performance, ridiculously shuffling about the stage in a tall cardboard box. That's how I feel in Lycra-less denim.

6. THE BIG GIRL'S SILK BLOUSE

Inspired by Lauren Hutton's effortless style and the romantic dressing-up days of the late 60s and 70s, as well as Maggie Gyllenhaal's wardrobe in the TV show *The Honourable Woman*, I felt the urge to buy a silk blouse. I've always been fond of sparkle; there's a healthy sprinkling of Lurex in my party drawer, but a silk blouse isn't something I'd ever considered. That was until I came across a gold Escada number for eight quid at a vintage fair. Outré 80s Escada had never been on my must-have list, but this second-hand silk blouse was grown-up, glamorous and, er, golden.

Silk is a lovely, luxurious fibre that at certain points in history – the grand old days in Rome when Emperor Caligula and his pals were draped in the stuff – cost more money than gold. As a woven fabric, it feels cool in summer and warm in winter, and hence comfortable to wear whatever the season. Silk's thermal properties can cause a bit of cling. But that's not a bad thing, is it? – just as long as you're wearing the right bra. Extravagant and decadent, an unbuttoned silk blouse was the perfect thing for slinking around Studio 54 in (though my guess is that was without a bra). A disco-tastic look revisited by Tom Ford at Gucci in the 1990s, when his superb collection of jewel-coloured silky shirts and velvet trousers grabbed the fashion world's attention. Personally, I prefer to play a super-shiny shirt off against something more low-key, like a pair of old ripped jeans. And that's probably why the big

girl's blouse always reminds me of Keith Richards, circa 1967, wearing his then girlfriend Anita Pallenberg's clothes. As the ageing rocker recalls in *Life*, 'Anita had a huge influence on the style of the times. She could put anything together and look good. I was beginning to wear her clothes most of the time. I would wake up and put on what was lying around. But it really pissed off Charlie Watts, with his walk-in cupboards of impeccable Savile Row suits, that I started to become a fashion icon for wearing my old lady's clothes.'

The grown-up gold blouse was just the start of my Silk Road. I now own several variations in navy, blush pink and sky blue, called upon for work events or disco nights when I'm looking to dress things up in a decadent fashion.

THREE OF THE BEST SILK BLOUSES

1. Equipment Slim Signature Shirt – the fashion world's favourite brand, started in 1976 by Christian Restoin (Carine Roitfeld's husband) and worn by film stars, including the late Lauren Bacall.

2. The Tucker tunic top – a simple style that looks brilliant with jeans, provides ease of movement and a subtle flash of colour. The sartorial equivalent of a chilled glass of wine on a rooftop terrace.

3. Winser London Lauren Silk Tunic & Tie – this stretch silk blouse has a detachable tie so that it can be worn with or without a pussy bow. And it's named after Lauren Hutton, of course.

7. THE KICK-ASS JACKET

One of the best fashion photographs, ever, is Helmut Newton's shot of *Le Smoking* for French *Vogue* in 1975. At the time, the image caused a sensation, as Colin McDowell points out in *Fashion Today*, 'Nice women did not wear the ambiguous smokings of Yves Saint Laurent ... And yet, both suit and image were an homage to the new female elegance – years before their time.' This kind of female elegance is commonplace today, and can be seen in numerous Parisian street-style shots of French *Vogue* editor-in-chief Emmanuelle Alt.

A sharp, kick-ass jacket slipped insouciantly over jeans, a T-shirt and a pair of spindly heels – whether it's black, white, leather or tweed – the mannish blazer is a steadfast component of the oh-so-chic French look. Alt's stripped-back style offers the perfect example of modern uniform dressing.

And another thing. I never really understood that whole 'It bag' phenomenon – or the *Sex and the City* designer shoe obsession, for that matter. I once visited an exhibition of 'crazy shoes' at the Museum of the Fashion Institute of Technology in New York and it felt like a trip to *Ripley's Believe It or Not*.

To me, a decent jacket feels like a wiser investment than any overpriced, look-at-me leather accessory that's going to spend more time in the cupboard than in use. The new super power dressing is much more subtle and softer round the edges, and it doesn't require an ostentatious display of wealth. Bring it on.

8. THE ESSENTIAL GREY TOP

I know that jersey sportswear is not everyone's cup of char, but simple pieces can sometimes have the greatest impact. When it comes to Wardrobe Glue, the essential grey T-shirt and the essential grey sweatshirt have superior sticking power. For those who prefer proper luxury, I give you the charcoal-grey cashmere sweater. All three of these are the kind of easy-going items that Jane Birkin has in her armoire – not young, free and bra-less Jane, but Jane now. Worn beneath a tuxedo or luxurious leather jacket, a simple T-shirt has excellent go-anywhere credentials and an innate ability to pull an outfit together. Similarly the chic sweatshirt or cashmere knit is an easy alternative to a jacket – one that can be rolled up and shoved into a bag – worn over a coloured pencil skirt it becomes the epitome of Casual Glamour. The shade of grey matters though; the tone has to be just right. Steely French hues and charcoals are much more flattering than pale dove greys. Lighter shades tend to drain the life out of an older complexion and are not the greatest compliment to gorgeous grey hair.

In the wrong hands, the essential grey top can appear all casual, no glamour. But as Céline designer Phoebe Philo has shown, elegant, modern sports-influenced fashion does have a place in the grown-up woman's wardrobe – the Céline designer lives in beautiful, sleek separates and sporty trainers. The key here is to temper the casual element with something really sharp. I've learnt that there are ways and

THE 10 BEST KICK-ASS JACKET MOMENTS

1

Patti Smith in a dishevelled white shirt, boyfriend jacket slung over her shoulder on the cover of *Horses*, 1975.

2

Lauren Hutton striding down the Tom Ford catwalk in 2011 in a brilliant white trouser suit, silk shirt and fedora.

3

Marlene Dietrich looking uber-feminine in trademark men's suit and jaunty beret during the Golden Age of Hollywood.

4

Dynasty-era Joan Collins in a bright-red, big-shouldered jacket and matching leather gloves. Clearly the hair and earrings are big too.

5

'It really does make you feel different, it changes gestures,' says Catherine Deneuve, forever fabulous in Yves Saint Laurent's *Le Smoking*.

6

Janelle Monae launches a debut album with a slick androgynous look and signature pompadour, 2010.

7

Chanel's tweed jacket with pockets and braid and gold buttons created during the designer's comeback after the Second World War in 1954, had its own exhibition in 2012.

8

Debbie Harry is oh-so-sexy in an oversized men's jacket, figure-hugging black dress and thigh-high boots, 1983.

9

Tilda Swinton looking like the Man Who Fell to Earth in Haider Ackermann, at the V&A's 'David Bowie Is' private view, 2013.

10

The Jagger Swagger: Bianca cool as fuck in a white YSL tuxedo and bowler hat, 1972.

there are ways to wear an essential grey top. To avoid straying into the territory of an overgrown teenager, here is my grown-up guide:

- Embrace proportion control by balancing an oversized top with more streamlined bottoms. A pair of slim trousers or straight-leg jeans should do the trick.

- Smarten up the jeans and t-shirt option by throwing on a kick-ass jacket.

- Heels or metallic flats are the perfect finishing touch and an easy way to avoid looking too dressed down.

- Crank up the wow-factor with a pair of fabulous Liz Taylor earrings, a gorgeous silk scarf or a top-notch party necklace.

9. THE GO-EVERYWHERE TUNIC DRESS

The Fashion Museum in Bath, England, has a Dress of the Year award. The inaugural prize went to Mary Quant for a grey wool pinafore in 1963 and every year since, a fashion expert has selected a contemporary frock to go on display at the museum. I'm still waiting for the call-up, but for modern-day versatility I'd choose the tunic dress. First introduced by Paul Poiret in the early 20th century, this style was popularised several decades later by Cristobal Balenciaga. Known for developing innovative shapes and silhouettes, in 1955

the Spanish designer showed a collection in Paris featuring a slim almost-to-the-knee, unbelted tunic over a matching sheath dress. Described by the fashion media as the 'event of the collection', Carmel Snow reported its significance in *Harper's Bazaar*: 'The future is never a matter for hazardous conjecture. He has a clear insight into the evolution of women's taste; and eventually that insight always proves true. This spring he launched a most important line, a long, supple tunic ...'

Of course, the dress of the year should offer year-round style. Last summer I bumped into doyenne of British fashion, Wendy Dagworthy, wearing a simple white tunic dress from Cos (the best place to find one on the high street, in my opinion), accessorised with a silver metal collar, stacks of trademark silver bangles and flat white leather sandals. Long grey hair in a topknot, she looked magnificent. Cool, chic and summery. And when I interviewed Wendy for this book, she was wearing a similar navy dress and a Holly Fulton Perspex necklace. I don't tend to unleash my varicose veins in summer, but as part of my journey to work involves riding a bike, in winter I'll often choose a tunic shape as an easy sartorial option. Fortunately all my frocks come in a modest just-above-the-knee length and can be worn with opaque tights so as not to scare the motorists. As retail guru Mary Portas concurs, 'If I only had space in my wardrobe for one dress, it would be a tunic style. You can throw this piece over a T-shirt, great hosiery or leggings. Every woman needs outfits that are fail-safe; throw-on and look fabulous in five minutes. I call it the No-Brainer.'

10. THE CHIC NOT CLICHÉD BRETON TOP

I love a good stripe. Maybe it's a growing-up-by-the-seaside thing, though to be honest, the only stripes I can recall from a childhood spent in Blackpool were those attached to deckchairs, or on the side of a stick of rock.

The Breton top originated in Brittany, in 1858, and started out as workwear for sailors. The wide boat neckline allowed the garment to be quickly pulled on over the head, while the broad horizontal stripes were easy to spot if a man fell overboard. Early mariners had 21 stripes; one for each of Napoleon's victories – until, of course, he met his match at Waterloo. By the 1920s, Chanel was promenading along the French Riviera in one. Having opened a boutique in Cannes in 1923, she quickly became immersed in Riviera chic and a year later designed sporty costumes, including bathing suits and striped tops, for the Ballet Russes performance of *Le Train Bleu* (the name of the overnight train that ran from Paris to the Riviera). As noted in Justine Picardie's biography, *Chanel: The Legend and the Life*, the stage curtain was painted by Picasso, a friend of Chanel's and consummate fan of the Breton stripe. It's a long way from the Cote d'Azur to the Fylde Coast, but Chanel's poor boy chic has always struck a chord with my working-class sensibilities.

It's easy to see that parallel lines can perk up any outfit; adding a smidgen of understated glamour to simple trousers and jeans. And take no notice of that nonsense about horizontal stripes – a top that fits well and is in proportion with the body is always flattering. But no need to go full-on French ingénue; I find a modern-day mash up – adding a floral-print skirt or pair of camouflage pants – is one of the best ways to wear a Breton. Jean Paul Gaultier has practically made a career out of playing with stripes, 'The shock of the way I mix patterns and fabrics can be disconcerting,' he told *Vogue* in 1984, 'but what I am trying to do is provoke new ideas about how pieces can be put together in different ways. I think this is a more modern way to wear clothes that in themselves are fairly classic.' And this theory still applies today. Standing in the middle of *The Fashion World of Jean Paul Gaultier* exhibition last year, I was reminded of the way Jenna Lyons mixes things up at J. Crew – as well as the longevity of the simple stripey T-shirt, 'My mother dressed me in sailor-striped sweaters,' says Gaultier. 'They go with everything, never go out of style, and probably never will.'

THREE OF THE BEST PLACES TO BUY A BRETON:

Petit Bateau – this popular French brand started out as a childrenswear label but the larger teen sizes proved so popular with adults, a grown-up range was eventually added. Good for marinières in many colours and Breton-with-a-twist creative collaborations.

Gap – one of my favourite stripy T-shirts is charcoal grey and royal blue with a fluorescent orange neckline and cost £2.99 in the Gap sale. I can't tell you how many times I wish I'd bought in bulk.

Saint James – as worn by Pablo Picasso, the manufacturer of the original French fisherman's tricot was founded in Normandy in 1850 and is still going strong and available online today.

11. THE GROWN-UP JUMPSUIT

Meet the new kid that's been around the block. Yep, I thought a pair of black trousers was the most timesaving garment, ever, until … The Return of the Jumpsuit. First worn during my 'futuristic period' and revisited last year, the all-black, all in one makes getting dressed a doddle. The new version is proper French work wear, purchased at an elevated price from Margaret Howell's MHL line, it is commonly referred to as the Industrial Onesie. The fabric is quite heavy duty and not really suitable for the summer months, otherwise I find I'm boiling in my boilersuit. And now, I want one in every available colour/fabric known to womankind. All that 'going to the loo is such a palaver' stuff is drivel. Believe me, I go a lot. Just be careful not to drop the arms down the toilet bowl, tie them in a loose knot across the lap and avoid weeing on your sleeves. It's simple.

'It's never too late to be what you might have been'
– George Elliot

Thelma Speirs

MILLINER, DJ AND FASHION MUSE, THELMA SPEIRS LIVES AND WORKS IN EAST LONDON.

'I used to do that granny chic thing, but when you're old enough to be a granny it doesn't work any more.'

ON BEING A MILLINER

It's brilliant. I always wanted to work in fashion and I always wanted to work by myself – well, with Paul (Bernstock, her business partner at Bernstock Speirs). We didn't have a business plan when we started out, we just muddled through. We didn't do it for the money. We did it for the freedom. I still find it exciting, I'm happy to be a part of it. Hats are pretty joyful – they're not much to do with anything but having fun and expressing yourself.

ON AGE

When I was young, if I saw older people out clubbing I thought they were just fantastic and sophisticated and glamorous. (They probably weren't even that old, maybe about 40.) I just really liked older women and the way they looked. I saw *The Graduate* and wanted to be Anne Bancroft. So getting older has never really bothered me. I feel quite good really, but at 55 I don't feel that old. I don't know if you ever do ...

ON DJING

It's such good fun. Princess Julia (the London DJ and music writer) got me into it. I didn't really know what to do and she said, 'Just press play.' It's such a nice thing to do, a bit like performing for shy people. To have everyone dancing and interacting with me because of the songs I pick is brilliant. I play quite camp things, the gays like it.

ON STYLE

I'm quite boyish really, but I can dress like a woman. I like elements of 1960s style and dressing up. When I was young I thought Liza Minnelli was fab, she would throw a bit of glitter at something and it would be all right.

ON GOING GREY

I went grey in my late 20s and liked it. I did try dyeing it brunette again once and really regretted it. I felt like I'd lost my look. People thought I was older than I was, but that didn't bother me because I'd always wanted to look older anyway.

ON RELAXING

I like challenging myself and I like a goal. I recently started running ... well, I'm on week two of the Couch-to-5K app. I like yoga and gardening and I'm learning to play the ukulele, I already have an electric guitar – I'd love to be in a band.

ON BOTOX

It's not for me. A few lines don't bother me and I think you have to be careful with procedures of this sort. What happens in America, in Hollywood, the pressure to look young is terrifying. I'm sure most female actors have had a bit of work done – women have always had a shit time on that front.

ON WHAT'S IMPORTANT

Creativity. Love. Friendship.

ON WHAT YOU'D SAY TO YOUR 15-YEAR-OLD SELF

Pursue your career and enjoy it ... which I did!

Cindy Joseph

FOUNDER OF THE COSMETIC LINE BOOM.
THE FORMER MAKE-UP ARTIST LIVES IN SAN
FRANCISCO AND TALKS REGULARLY ON THE
SUBJECT OF PRO-AGEING.

*'It's crazy, people pay thousands of
dollars for photographs of beautiful
older women, like Georgia O'Keefe,
and then they look in the mirror, see
one wrinkle and freak out.'*

ON PRO-AGE

My Pro-Age campaign is about saying 'enough already'. We're led to believe that life is an upward journey that reaches a midlife crescendo – the prime of life – and, after that, the future's doomed. I'm like the kid in the 'Emperor's New Clothes' who tells everyone the king is naked. I'm just telling the truth about women, beauty and age. We've been told a load of crock and now we want the truth. Women are judged heavily on their looks; when you're young and beautiful you're perceived as having value – and that, somehow, we lose value as we age. That's total make-believe; after all, matriarchs of families are highly respected. We need to feel beautiful all the way through life. I'm 64 and I know I'm getting better, smarter, wiser, more experienced in every area.

ON LOOKING FABULOUS

Fabulousness is in the eye of the beholder. We all have a different viewpoint and we all have opinions. There is a perception of beauty in our society pedalled by the media and I think that's what everyone is rebelling against. I'm not interested in looking younger, I want to look healthy and radiant. I want to look like me – and I want to be a positive role model for younger women.

ON YOUNG EQUALS ATTRACTIVE

If a woman buys into the idea of needing to look younger, it doesn't work. Trying to hide our age just makes us look desperate. We need to tweak our thought process. Women who live in fear are not attractive, happy women are attractive. If you feel good inside, it creates a charismatic attractiveness.

ON THE OLD LADY REVOLUTION

It's about time. What the women of
the Boomer Generation are doing is
unprecedented. We have reinvented every
decade of our lives and are continuing
to do so in our 60s and 70s – starting
new careers, going back to college –
we're doing stuff differently to the
previous generation. We're a new wave
of older women and retailers have finally
recognised that.

ON WHAT YOU'D SAY TO YOUR 15-YEAR-OLD SELF

Live a pleasurable life. Be as nice as you
can be. Love yourself. You are worth
falling in love with. Wouldn't it have been
amazing if we'd heard that at 15?

Baroness Susan Greenfield

PROFESSOR OF PHARMACOLOGY AT OXFORD UNIVERSITY, BROADCASTER, WRITER AND AUTHOR OF SEVERAL BOOKS, INCLUDING *MIND CHANGE*.

'I wouldn't want to be young again; maturity and experience give you confidence and that is wonderfully liberating.'

ON THE BABY BOOMER GENERATION

The Baby Boomers are redefining old age. We're working longer – I'm 64 and I truly don't feel it – and we're healthier, I have the same lifestyle as in my 40s and 50s. My generation was the first to be brought up by the welfare state; injections; stay-at-home mums; higher education. There was an emphasis on health and wellbeing; we were more accounted for than the Fast Food Generation. The Baby Boomers had a very privileged little window and those expectations carry on.

ON AGE

Obviously what I don't welcome is the notion of becoming weaker. But ageing is just maturing and evolving. Sometimes people lose their sparkle. It happens at different ages. In my case I'm trying to cure Alzheimer's so that challenge keeps me young. My colleagues are all young, so no one's moaning about hip replacements.

Even my mum, who is 87 and goes line-dancing, talks about old people. She is very agile physically and mentally, and that's rubbed off on me. I'd go nuts on a beach. I love doing things: thinking, writing, working.

ON SOCIAL NETWORKING

I'm not a social networker. If people want to spend their life on the planet ranting on blogs, that's fine, but we end up reporting what we're doing rather than actually having the experience. I enjoy my 3D real life and would rather have 10 real friends than 50 who act like an audience.

ON BEING IN THE PUBLIC EYE

On the whole, I ignore it. Unless you're the queen or David Attenborough, the press loves bad news and bad things, so it's best not to read it. Although 99 per cent of what's said about me is actually quite nice, I don't make it a priority to pay attention to it. You are aware as a woman in the public eye that people are going to comment on your clothes rather than your track record. I don't mind when it's for a fashion book, but when it's a national newspaper talking about your appearance, it's demeaning.

ON KEEPING FIT

Health is important to me. There's that Morecambe and Wise quote: 'There's one thing I want to do before I die and that's live a long time.' I do Pilates once a week and play squash. I'm not hugely sporty and I know it's a cliché, but you do always feel better after sport; it's important to stay physically fit and strong.

ON SUSAN GREENFIELD-STYLE

I have constraints but they're not age-related. I still wear short skirts, which might horrify some people, but I wouldn't show acres of flesh. That doesn't look good at any age. It's important to me to look healthy and well groomed; not bitten-down fingernails and dirty, frizzy hair – I'm aware now if I need a manicure.

ON WHAT YOU'D SAY TO YOUR 15-YEAR-OLD SELF

Be yourself. Be consistent. Be open and honest with people – if they don't like it, don't get upset. You should be able to look yourself in the eye.

LIFESTYLE FOREVER: LOOKING AFTER BODY AND MIND IS IMPORTANT TOO

PILATES IS THE NEW CLUBBING

You are never too old for Pilates – and there are loads of videos of pensioners on YouTube to prove it. I started at 48 and there's a man who goes to the same studio as me who's as fit as a fiddle at 81. Often associated with the 'Yummy Mummy Tummy', I think Pilates is better for older people. Without wanting to go all Goop-y Gwyneth Paltrow; my local studio Artichoke Pilates is freakin' awesome. I love going there because it's full of fantastic, like-minded people of a certain vintage, very sociable and loads of fun.

Pilates is the new clubbing. It's also good for strengthening and toning muscles and improving posture and flexibility; I got into it because I have a dodgy back and my Pilates pal Janey has a shoulder problem and neither of us wanted to be subject to the condition we've nicknamed 'Croning' (the hunched-over posture associated with osteoporosis). Once a week, I also go to a mat class; mainly to have a lie down and a laugh. The 64-year-old Polish tutor Bagusha has an amazing physique and a unique way with words. Thus, tilting the pelvis is called 'Michael Jackson Hips', and there's also the 'George Clooney on the Beach' manoeuvre (spine stretch: shoulders back, chest lifted). While it has its humorous side, Pilates can also provide psychological strength. Joseph Pilates had to overcome lots of struggles in his life, including being interned during the First World War, in a prison camp on the Isle of Man (this is where he developed his ideas). His philosophy is based on the principle that having more control over the body allows you to feel more relaxed and in control of other aspects of your life. And stretch …

135

GIVE YOUR BRAIN
A REST

I downloaded the Head Space app when the constant chatter inside my head and online was becoming a bit much. My work–life–blogging balance was out of kilter and I felt like I needed to take five. I know, I know, why not just step away from the iPhone? 'Mindfulness was originally part of Buddhist philosophy and it's increasingly seen as a quick fix to an excess of technology,' says Harriet Griffey, author of *I Want to Be Calm: How to De-stress*. 'But to be truly effective it needs to become a way of being, rather than something that's done for 10 minutes once a day and forgotten about.' For that reason (as well as the fact that every time I listened to the app I fell asleep) I started going to a drop-in session at a local yoga studio. 'It's not some inexplicable mumbo-jumbo,' adds Harriet, 'There are physical benefits from practising mindfulness. Calming the mind can help slow the secretion of stress hormones which reduces physical damage to the body.'

DID SOMEBODY
MENTION THE
MENOPAUSE?

They did, so I asked Leah Hardy, co-author of *Your Hormone Doctor* for some expert advice:

'As we get older, our hormones change, both in the rollercoaster ride before the menopause that's called the peri-menopause, and at the menopause itself.

It's so inevitable, the menopause could perhaps be described as the defining female experience. Unlike pregnancy and childbirth, it's something we all go through – provided we live long enough. For generations, that wasn't the case. Now, with life expectancy closer to 90 than 80, the menopause may arrive at just over the half-way mark in life.

Yes, menopausal changes are dramatic, and for some women, they can be a challenge. Hot flushes anyone? However, there are plenty of ways to reduce the flushes, muscle and bone loss, anxiety and the other symptoms women fear. Start with good nutrition. Eat plenty of vegetables, fruit, and protein, and as little in the way of sugar and processed carbs as you can bear. Exercise becomes non-negotiable if you want to look good, and more importantly stay vital, independent and enjoy life as you get older.

Walking and weights work for bones, mental health, muscles and happiness. Add Pilates or yoga for flexibility, toned limbs and serenity. Cut down on stress, keep up your social life, be open-minded, laugh and find a passion – be it a house, a job, a university course or a partner. And stop the 'hor-moaning' – the whingeing about young people/your feet/technology/digestion, that gets curiously tempting as you get older, but makes you sound and feel hideously ancient. Remember, we hear everything we say about ourselves, and our own negative comments can make us feel as low as if someone else is insulting us. Our health depends on positivity. When we frown we send signals to our brain that makes us

HARRIET GRIFFEY'S SIX TOP TIPS FOR LIVING A MINDFUL LIFE:

1

Do one thing at a time rather than multitasking: multitasking is the antithesis of mindfulness!

2

Practice mindful breathing techniques every day: this will help create the pause you need, when you need it, in a busy day.

3

Try not to stand in judgement, of yourself or others: acknowledge your thoughts and let them go.

4

Respond rather than react: take five mindful breaths if you need to take a moment, and then respond.

5

Be aware that physical sensations – lack of sleep, hunger, dehydration – can all make the body more stressed, which can hinder feelings of calm.

6

At least once a day, acknowledge three good things in your life and give thanks for their presence.

more prone to depression, but if we smile at ourselves we get the same hormonal boost as if someone else is smiling at us.

Style-wise, hormonal changes, particularly loss of oestrogen, affect the skin, making it drier, thinner and even paler, as the cells that produce colour depend on oestrogen. A good hydrating moisturiser and cream blusher are your friend now. Hair may become curlier and coarser, or it may become finer and you might notice less of it. Work with it. Add layers, grow your hair if you like it long, colour it if you want, or embrace the grey. Lashes and brows may thin. If this bothers you, try a lash and brow serum and a great mascara. Your body shape will change, just as it did at puberty, but in the opposite direction. Hormones now drive fat away from your hips and thighs and towards your middle. These can present fashion challenges but also new opportunities. Your wasp waist may be no more, but your narrow hips and lean legs could look amazing in skinny jeans. Experiment to find the style to suit your evolving shape. If you lose bone you can find yourself getting shorter, and thicker-waisted, and, much worse, eventually become weak and lack mobility. It's vital to prevent this. Keep your skeleton strong with weight-bearing exercise.

You might want to consider hormone replacement therapy, either with conventional HRT or with bio-identical hormones, which are recognised by your body as the same as your own natural hormones. It's a decision to take with your doctor, but according to the British Menopause Society, HRT prescribed before

the age of 60 has more benefits than risks. Hormone supplements can keep skin and hair thick and limit shape changes as well as boosting bones.

The good news is that, as women hit the menopause, hormones stablise. Many women love the freedom that comes when the tyranny of the monthly cycle is over. The hormonal wild ride that can cause PMT and peri-menopausal depression and anxiety simply stops, and those problems often fade away. Indeed, it's common for menopausal women to experience a surge of creativity, happiness and confidence, and feel much less bothered about what other people think of them. Style can become more individual, more adventurous. This can be an amazing time.

As women in mid-life, we are the new power generation. We have demographics on our side. We are more prominent in politics and business. We are very much engaged with life and we like to look good – not just 'good for our age'. Right now, one in four women is over 50. In five years' time, one in three will be. We still like to look good. Women over 50 account for 41 per cent of the total spend on make up, skincare and toiletries and we are still loving our lives. Many studies have found women's lives improve after the menopause. The 2002 Jubilee Report (a major survey of women's wellbeing) found that 65 per cent of women over 50 said they were happier than before. When it came to health, 76 per cent said they were healthier, and 75 per cent said they had more fun. And nothing is chicer than that!

LIFESTYLE FOREVER: LOOKING AFTER BODY AND MIND IS IMPORTANT TOO.

139

HOTSPOTS

THAT IS MY AGE: FAVOURITE PLACES

Iris Apfel is right. You do need to get out there, stay current and stay interested. The two cities I spend the most time in are London and New York (free accommodation with Manhattan Brother helps). There are so many fantastic places to go and things to do, here are a few of my favourites. Most of my recommendations include pitstops for food and drink. That's how me and the Blow Widower roll. We love a good walk and a quality snack.

LONDON

FIVE FABULOUS PLACES

1. SOMERSET HOUSE

The home of London Fashion Week is so much nicer when the fashion crowd have flown off to Milan. This gorgeous, golden Portland stone building sits in a beautiful location (the home of a former Tudor palace) right next to the River Thames. There's always an exhibition or gig worth seeing, and on a hot sunny day, I can highly recommend relaxing in the grand courtyard with a bowl of garlicky gazpacho and a sandwich from Fernandez & Wells, watching the kids (and the odd adult) splashing through the fountains.

2. BRIXTON VILLAGE

Brixton Market has gone upmarket. What was once Granville Arcade is now called Brixton Village. There are loads of fantastic places to eat, though. After a trip to the Ritzy Cinema, we usually end up at French & Grace for a halloumi wrap and the best affogato in town. The hot drinks at Federation Coffee on Fifth Avenue are just as good as anything you'd buy in Manhattan; I can never manage a cup of Joe without one of their delicious Anzac biscuits on the side. And there's also a small selection of vintage shops and stores worth rummaging in.

3. THE GROWN-UP SHOPPING TRIANGLE

If I have time to kill between meetings in central London, I like to do a spot of fantasy shopping at Liberty or Fenwick of Bond Street. Minus the crowds both places offer a near-perfect, grown-up retail experience: beautifully edited fashion (Fenwick has an excellent lingerie department and a Blink concession where I get my eyebrows threaded), a decent cafe and tons of brilliant gift ideas. And most importantly, there's a Cos in between.

4. COLUMBIA ROAD FLOWER MARKET

There comes a time in life when you'd rather stay in on a Saturday night watching crap TV than head to an over-crowded bar or restaurant. The good news is that this makes getting up early on a Sunday morning, to visit a poncey flower/farmer's market, all the more easier. We always grab a coffee at Beagle Cafe next to Hoxton Station, some cut flowers from Columbia Road market and then head to Calvert Avenue or Redchurch Street for a quick browse around the shops, and a spot of lunch at Pizza East or Leila's nearby.

5. LONDON'S LOVELY PARKS

One of the best things about London is the amount of green space. It has the most impressive parks of any major city.

Including Regents Park, where Colin Firth goes for a stroll in *The King's Speech* and Richmond Park, which has proper Royal connections and is the perfect place for picnics, bike rides and deer-spotting. But my favourite green space is much closer to home. South London's Brockwell Park has a wilder side, a walled flower garden and an open-air lido. We often go there for a Sunday stroll prior to stocking up on vegetables at the farmer's market in Herne Hill. (Could I sound more middle class?) On the corner there's Bleu vintage furniture shop for mid-century bits and pieces, where we often add to our ever-expanding collection of second-hand globes.

THREE FABULOUS PLACES TO EAT AND TWO DECENT CENTRAL LONDON COFFEE SHOPS

1. MORITO

This top tapas bar on Exmouth Market is the little sister of Moro and offers more choice for vegetarians.

2. JOSÉ

Combine a trip to Tanner Street market or the White Cube gallery with some more top tapas on Bermondsey Street.

3. MILDRED'S

The best vegetarian restaurant in town. Check out the burger of the day and chips with basil mayo – but save some room for the white chocolate cheesecake.

4. TWO GROWN-UP COFFEE SHOPS

Flat White on Berwick Street and Kaffeine on Great Titchfield Street.

NEW YORK

FIVE FABULOUS PLACES

1. THE HIGH LINE

When I stay with Manhattan Brother, I have a rule: to visit somewhere new in New York. Somewhere I've never been before. Sounds easy, I know, but he's lived there for 15 years and I'm quite content drinking coffee and walking up and down the High Line. This landscaped, old industrial railway line is the bee's knees. Every city should have one. For refreshments, I can recommend: Stone Street Coffee (9th Avenue, between 18th and 19th streets). There's a lively speakeasy called Bathtub Gin behind this local coffee shop at the weekend; the Half King pub (West 23rd Street) for a beer and a burger, or the Brass Monkey (55 Little West 12th Street).

2. BROOKLYN MUSEUM

Far less crowded than Manhattan's Museum Mile, this wonderful gallery is well worth jumping on the subway for. I've seen some brilliant exhibitions here including: a Keith Haring retrospective, The Fashion World of Jean Paul Gaultier, photography by Annie Liebowitz and Ron Mueck's fantastic sculptures. Afterwards, I go for a walk in Prospect Park and wander around Park Slope staring longingly at the beautiful Brooklyn Brownstones like the property porn addict that I am. I love a bit of property porn and in a parallel universe this is where I live.

3. AROUND UNION SQUARE & OVER TO 5TH AVENUE

In winter, I like to grab a cup of hot apple cider at the farmer's market in Union Square and then go for a walkabout in my Polar Vortex Parka. ABC Carpet & Home store on Broadway nearby is always worth a visit. Not to mention the ABC Cocina restaurant. And if you walk across to 5th Avenue and down, there are smaller scale versions of all the stores without the crowds, including: J. Crew, Gap, Kate Spade, Madewell, Coach, Anthropologie, Banana Republic, Nike, New Balance. Then finish off the tour with a walk back up towards the iconic Flatiron Building.

4. NEW YORK FLEA MARKETS

Forget 5th Avenue, I'm much happier rummaging through other people's junk. Now that Chelsea Antiques Garage has closed down (for prime real estate reasons, natch), head up to Hell's Kitchen for some outdoor action or over to the fancy pants Brooklyn Flea, which also has an outpost in Park Slope.

5. THE JACQUELINE KENNEDY ONASSIS RESERVOIR IN CENTRAL PARK

Get away from the tourists and the knackered, old horses pulling carts (which Mayor Bill de Blasio is trying to ban), and hire a bike from the Citibike stand just across from Columbus Circle. Or go for a walk around the Jacqueline Kennedy Onassis Reservoir. Whatever the season, this is a lovely spot. Last year we spotted a black squirrel (who knew?) and a body being dragged out of the lake. This is where the action is.

FIVE FABULOUS PLACES TO EAT

1. OVEST PIZZATECA, CHELSEA
Good pizzas, reasonably priced; low-key glamour. Well, I once saw John Turturro here.

2. CLAUDETTE, WASHINGTON SQUARE
French cuisine is back in NYC and this is the chicest place for brunch.

3. BAR PRIMI, BOWERY
Newish Italian spot from the chef Andrew Carmellini (owner of The Dutch and Locanda Verde). Delicioso!

4. WESTVILLE, CHELSEA
Ari from *Advanced Style* introduced me to this great lunch/brunch spot. There are a couple of other restaurants dotted around Manhattan.

5. TAMARIND, TRIBECA
A posh Indian serving the best food ever. Don't get me started on Midtown's 'Curry in a Hurry'.

AND A BAR WITH A SPECTACULAR VIEW

GAONNURI, BROADWAY
This mid-town Korean restaurant on the 39th floor offers spectacular views of the Manhattan skyline. You feel like you're in a movie.

FUTURE FABSTER

Lauren Laverne

LAUREN BEGAN HER CAREER IN A 90S INDIE BAND AND MOVED INTO JOURNALISM AND BROADCASTING. SHE'S NOW AN ACCLAIMED BBC 6 MUSIC DJ, TV PRESENTER AND WRITER.

'There is still a lot of prejudice against older people, which makes me as angry as everyone else, but I hope and believe that things are changing.'

ON BEING IN THE PUBLIC EYE

I work at the BBC every day doing my 6 Music radio show, so the paparazzi might catch a snap of me as I come in and out, but not so often that I have to think about it! TV presenter Fearne Cotton is in the studio around the corner and she has to give much more consideration to what she wears! Mostly I just dress to please myself.

ON AGE

I'm 36, and very comfortable with my own style and with my age (not that I think about it all that much). I feel pretty positive about ageing. There are so many fantastic, inspiring role models around.

ON THE OLD LADY REVOLUTION

Boring answer (I'm the daughter of a sociologist, sorry!) I think it's down to population dispersal. The baby boomer is ageing and still dominating the consumer market, so ageing was bound to be rebranded as positive. That's quite a dry way of looking at it, though I'm really glad it's happening, and I do think it will change people's attitudes. Once people who can sell you stuff realise the potential of any given market, they tend not to want to stop selling them things!

ON WRITING ABOUT STYLE (LAUREN IS A REGULAR CONTRIBUTOR TO SEVERAL WOMEN'S MAGAZINES AND WRITES A LIFESTYLE COLUMN FOR THE *OBSERVER* NEWSPAPER)

I really enjoy writing about style, clothes and our relationship with them – they have a huge influence on how you feel and are a great way to express yourself. Fashion is not quite so much my bag. I like it so long as it's fun and beautiful, but the aspects of it that are exploitative, or make people feel bad about themselves in some way … that's a no from me.

ON LAUREN LAVERNE-STYLE

I think my attitude to how I look has improved as I've got older – I'm more accepting of myself, as clichéd as that sounds. I don't think my style has changed much at all. I still have as much fun dressing up as I ever did. Probably more so, as I no longer feel the need to wear what other people approve of so much. I'm not worried about wearing the 'right' thing any more. For me, dressing is more about attitude and who you are than how old. Having said that, I prefer to be a little more covered up than I used to be in my 20s, maybe a little more comfortable.

I'm happier in a brogue than a huge heel these days. I tend to change what I wear completely rather than water it down (I can't get on with low heels at all for example – they remind me of the Queen Mum!).

ON WHAT YOU'D SAY TO YOUR 15-YEAR-OLD SELF

Please be kinder to yourself. And hang in there, it's all going to be GREAT.

P.S

WHO ARE YOU CALLING INVISIBLE?

From Miuccia Prada to Mary Berry, women of all ages like to look around for intelligent, accomplished role models, other women of substance that they can look up to. The problem is that although *Generation FAB* is visible in the workplace, out on the pavements and on the internet, we're a lot less visible in Parliament and on the BBC (*Bake Off* being an exception). I strongly believe that we need to fight back against this invisibility thing – because it's rude and ridiculous and older women deserve respect.

Yes, we are viewed differently by men – and that's down to evolution and biology – but it doesn't mean we have to lose our voice, or our allure. Though to be honest, if being viewed differently means not having random men shouting,

'I wish I was your saddle' every time I cycle down the road, then I'm quite happy with that. What I don't like is the idea of being written off as being past it while grey-haired male counterparts are viewed as having knowledge, experience and wisdom. Or the fact that to remain in the limelight, talented women are expected not to show any signs of ageing. It's just not on. It's been enough of a struggle for women in general to obtain positions of power and responsibility, why should this be taken away when we get older?

The Old Lady Revolution has already started. Let's raise awareness of women who are in their prime. This is not the invisibility age, this is the VISIBILITY age.

Older women of the world unite and take over!

SIX BEAUTY EXPERTS
BEST-EVER PRODUCTS

As I wouldn't want to leave you feeling short-changed by a chapter that reads like Beauty Advice For Dummies, I've spoken to six of the best beauty, health and wellbeing experts to pick their brains and find out their favourite products. Just remember, less is more!

RUBY HAMMER
has worked in the beauty industry for over 25 years and is one of the best-known make-up artists in the UK. She describes being awarded an MBE by the queen as 'the highlight of my career'. Here are some of her favourite products:

CLARINS DOUBLE SERUM (COMPLETE AGE CONTROL CONCENTRATE)
Love the smell of this serum and how it feels on the skin. I layer everything else on top of this product – it takes care of hydration, lines, firmness – it's fantastic, I haven't stopped using it since it first launched.

BOURJOIS 123 PERFECT CC CREAM
This is one of my favourite CC (colour correcting) creams. It's easy to apply; use it as you would a moisturiser and blend it into the nooks and crannies around your nose. It's not too thick or heavy but offers great coverage, conceals dark spots and is SPF15. And it's reasonably priced too.

MAC BLOT POWDERS
These pressed powders come in various shades and are the best for getting rid of excess shine without leaving a cakey film on the skin. They're fantastic on the T-zone before a selfie!

DIOR 5 COULEURS EYE SHADOW PALETTES

This is my go-to palette, I've been using one (not the same one!) since the start of my career and it can create a multitude of looks and stop you getting stuck in a rut. I have a soft spot for the Beige Masai 705. Dior has reformulated this whole range and I love the new streamlined packaging and the great new formula and texture. Another favourite is BAR 056; this palette is good for everyday needs and will help you achieve the ultimate smoky eye.

BENEFITS THEY'RE REAL! MASCARA

I love the fact that this mascara gives you a false eyelashes effect. The brush is specially designed to catch every lash – even those hard to reach short ones.

CLINIQUE CHUBBY STICKS MOISTURIZING LIP COLOUR BALM

I love the fat twist-up lip crayons that are available now in pretty much all ranges; from expensive brands like Sisley to cheaper ones like Barry M. No sharpening needed and they're so easy to use. I'll go with Clinique Chubby Sticks as Clinique were the first to kick this trend off and they come in great colours.

SARA RAEBURN

is a make-up artist with a career spanning over 30 years; she has worked with many stars and supermodels including Isabella Rosselini, Kate Moss, Gwyneth Paltrow and Helena Bonham Carter, and is co-founder of the website *Expert Beauty Face*.

AURELIA PROBIOTIC SKINCARE MIRACLE CLEANSER

Ruby and I call ourselves the scrubbers, we're both really into skincare and cleansing. I like to use a cloth cleanser (on the days I'm not using my Clarisonic) and this is really effective and smells amazing.

STUDIO 10 AGE DEFY SKIN PERFECTOR

This is a make-up compact that corrects, conceals and covers up age spots, pigmentation dark circles and redness. I use it to retouch the bits of my complexion that I want to cover and then swish a little Bare Minerals through the T-Zone of my face for a translucent glow. On the go, I carry Nars Radiant Creamy Concealer.

SMASHBOX BROW TECH TRIO AND BROW TECH TO GO

Eyebrows lift and frame the eyes and are vital to the proportion of the face. I have both powder and a pencil. I carry the pencil in my handbag for quick application and use the powder at home, when I can use my magnifying mirror.

LANCÔME HYPNÔSE MASCARA

I like to be able to play with the mascara to create long, separated lashes. This is good for building volume without the clumpiness.

CLINIQUE'S CHUBBY STICK CHEEK COLOUR BALM

A soupçon of colour on the cheeks lifts the complexion and brightens the eyes. Cream blushers enhance more mature skin and these sticks go on easily, blend well and look translucent on naked skin.

CHANEL COROMANDEL PERFUME

I think of perfume as part of my personality, part of my style. This is my signature scent and I get so many compliments when I wear it.

JANE CUNNINGHAM

is a beauty writer and founder of *British Beauty Blogger* **and** *The Beauty Plus* **websites.**

LANOLIPS LEMONAID BALM

The genius of this luscious little tube is that it's filled with exfoliating balm (containing Lanolin) that leaves your lips conditioned and smooth. I use it overnight to be lipstick ready at dawn.

DECIEM HAND CHEMISTRY

Of all the hand creams I've ever used, this one is the most effective. Light, quickly absorbed and with incredible results in a couple of weeks in terms of hydrating, smoothing and brightening the skin, you've got a little mushroom extract (Tremella Fuciformis Sporocarp) that's shown to be 400 times more hydrating than Hyaluronic Acid. Let's give thanks for this.

AROMATHERAPY ASSOCIATES DEEP RELAX BATH & SHOWER OIL

This is the most beautiful blend of relaxing aromatherapy oils (vetivert, camomile and sandalwood) and it does the trick before bedtime if you're stressed. Nothing makes you look and feel more vibrant than a good night's sleep.

CHARLOTTE TILBURY ROCK 'N' KOHL EYE PENCIL

From sparkling violet, moody grey and deepest black, these are the best and softest kohl pencils in the business. They can be used on the inner and outer rims, and you are never, ever too old to rock a sexy liner.

IMEDEEN PRIME RENEWAL SKINCARE TABLETS

I wasn't a believer in skin supplements until I tried these – over a year on and I'm still taking them. You won't see anything radical, but I am convinced enough (that it helps with skin hydration and softness all over the body, as well as the face) to continue using them as part of my beauty routine.

CLARINS SUPER RESTORATIVE NIGHT CREAM

Formulated for older skin, and also menopausal skin, this is a luxury buy that will push back the hydration into your skin. Giving a boost to sluggish cells and a kick to collagen production capabilities, it brings back skin vibrancy and softness, which will also soften lines.

VICCI BENTLEY

is an award-winning beauty writer and cosmetics industry expert with over 40 years' experience. Her specialist subjects are skincare and perfume.

CHANEL LES BEIGES HEALTHY GLOW MULTI-COLOUR

The light-reflecting powders in this genius Chanel palette have just enough pigment to give skin a healthy glow, but are translucent so blend seamlessly. I use the palest as an invisible highlight on cheekbones and brow bones, the rose pink for a healthy tinge on cheek apples and the golden tan as a 'halo' over my brow close to the hairline and along my jawline.

CLARISONIC CLEANSING BRUSH

I swear by this. Based on toothbrush technology, sonic brushes really do leave skin looking sparkling clean and feeling incredibly soft. Their gentle de-flaking action totally replaces the need for other forms of exfoliation and their pore-cleansing ability is unrivalled. Gentle brushing boosts microcirculation, leaving skin that bit plumper, firmer and glowier.

DR BRANDT PORES NO MORE

You'd think that shiny open pores are kid's stuff, wouldn't you? But when oestrogen

leaves the house, the resulting slump in collagen production means that pores slacken too. This slightly tinted mousse-like primer keeps make-up looking fresher for longer and makes bare skin look smoother too.

E45 INTENSE RECOVERY LOTION
Body skin can get chronically dry post menopause, especially in thin zones like shins. I slather this on to soothe and prevent itchiness, especially when the central heating's on throughout the winter. It's cheap as chips too.

COLOR WOW ROOT COVER UP
Miracle powder you brush on to cover grey root regrowth between colour appointments. A total revolution! Allows me to go for almost eight weeks before I need a tint. Great natural-looking colour selection, waterproof and doesn't rub off on the pillow like some of the sprays.

X5 MAGNIFYING MIRROR
Sad, I know. But essential for the reading glasses generation, if you don't want your make-up to look as if you've chucked it at your face from across the room. Use the scary magnifying side to do fiddly stuff like mascara, liner, brow-work, then check the overall effect with the regular side.

MAK GILCHRIST
is a 'forty-fucking-nine' year-old model turned guerilla gardener. As well as appearing in numerous Chanel perfume ads, she is one of the founders of the Edible Bus Stop project, a social enterprise committed to turning unused local land into community gardens.

STAY OUT OF THE SUN
No really, STAY OUT OF THE SUN! Never compromise on having the highest sunblock you can on your face. My favourite sunblock by far is Korres Sunscreen Face Cream Yoghurt. It doesn't block your pores and isn't greasy.

JASON POWERSMILE WHITENING ALL NATURAL TOOTHPASTE
Contains no harsh chemicals, preservatives, artificial colours, sweeteners or gluten, unlike 'normal' toothpastes. I don't understand why anyone would use toothpaste that contains all that rubbish, when this has great whitening results.

JURLIQUE ROSE HAND CREAM
A bit of a treat, as it's not cheap but it is very, very good. I put it on at night just before I go to bed. I'm always gardening and need to look after my hands.

DR. HAUSCHKA QUINCE DAY CREAM FOR THE FACE

A lovely light and effective moisturiser for slightly dry skin. Sits well under make-up, it's organic, smells great and has no chemicals; win win win.

LIZ EARLE SKIN REPAIR MOISTURISER

I have a variety of moisturisers on my bathroom shelf as I like to switch them around. This is an old favourite; it smells nice, leaves your skin feeling hydrated and absorbs well.

KORRES WILD ROSE 24-HOUR MOISTURISING AND BRIGHTENING CREAM

Unlike many moisturisers for dry skin, this does not leave the skin looking oily. The Korres brand has strong ethics and delivers great products. This also smells lovely which, by now, you will have guessed is a strong factor in why I like my products.

TISH JETT

is an American fashion journalist and blogger and author of *Forever Chic*. She has lived in Paris for over 25 years and is perfectly placed to spill the, er, French beans.

RETACNYL

A 0.05 per cent prescription Retin A–trinitrine product. This is the most powerful product that exists, according to all the dermatologists and plastic surgeons with whom I spoke. From personal experience of more than 20 years of use, I can assure you it's a miracle in a tube.

CLARINS BAUME BEAUTÉ ECLAIR

This wonderful cream keeps its promise to 'tighten and brighten'. Used over one's moisturiser and under make-up, it gives that glow that one sees on the red carpet. It is also a two-for-one in that it doubles as a mask. Leave on for 15 minutes, rinse and voilà – the skin looks radiant.

VICHY 3 EN 1 PURETÉ THERMALE

Recommended to me by the most revered facialist in Paris, who also happens to have her own line of very expensive products, as the best product for cleansing the face and I think she's right. It is particularly efficacious for removing eye make-up.

TERRACOTTA COMPACT POWDER BY GUERLAIN

This is *every* Frenchwoman's secret for looking healthy and rested. It gives a glow and a slight *bronzage* to the visage, and comes in every imaginable shade for all skin colours. I would suggest that when buying this product ask for expert help choose the right colour for your complexion.

EUCERIN HYALURON FILLER

This is two moisturizing products. It's the hyaluronic acid that makes all the difference. These come recommended by my French dermatologist and, in the almost two years I've used it, I can see a difference in the texture of my skin.

GOMMAGE SURFIN PHYSIOLOGIQUE DE LA ROCHE-POSAY

A gentle, extra-fine facial exfoliant. It's my latest discovery and it is probably the best facial scrub I have ever used.

ABOUT THE AUTHOR

Alyson Walsh is a freelance fashion journalist and author of the celebrated blog *That's Not My Age*. She writes for the *Guardian* and *FT's How To Spend It, Saga Magazine* and *allaboutyou.com*. The former fashion editor of *Good Housekeeping* magazine strongly believes that you don't have to have youth to have style.

ABOUT THE ILLUSTRATOR

Leo Greenfield studied art and fashion at the Victorian College of the Arts, Australia. His projects have been exhibited in galleries in Australia and France and have gained him invitations to international Fashion Weeks in Sydney, Paris and London, and contributing to leading fashion magazines. Major commissions for Leo include; *Australian Vogue, Sunday Style* and *Cult Magazine*.

THANK YOU

A very special thank you to all the people who loyally follow *That's Not My Age* and have helped make this happen. To all the truly inspirational women interviewed and mentioned in this book. To my gorgeous friend Emma Marsden who convinced me that I should write the damn thing in the first place and supported me throughout – even on the hysterical days. My brilliant boss Katharine Boxall for her constant back-up and sense of humour in adversity. To Vicci Bentley and Leah Hardy for their words and wisdom; Brenda Polan and Navaz Baltiwalla for their expert advice and professional proof-reading skills. Thanks to my Publisher Kate Pollard at Hardie Grant for her vision, and Leo Greenfield for his wonderful illustrations. And the biggest thanks of all goes to my beloved Paul (Mr *That's Not My Age*) for being a fantastic editor-in-chief and very best friend. I would be feral without him.

Thanks to all the people whose quotes I've nabbed and also to the following publications:

Guardian – for the Emma Thompson quote in the Introduction
New York Times – Harold Koda quote in How to do Boho
Guardian – Jane Birkin quote in Six Stylish Sports Shoe Moments
Saga magazine – my Mary Berry interview first appeared here
Yes Please, Harper Collins – Amy Poehler quote in Never Mind the Botox
Icons of Fashion: Prestel Prada quote in An Outstanding Coat
Elle.com – Jean Paul Gaultier quote in Chic not Clichéd Breton Tops

INDEX

Style Forever by Alyson Walsh

First published in 2015 by Hardie Grant Books

Hardie Grant Books (UK)
5th & 6th Floors
52-54 Southwark Street
London SE1 1UN
www.hardiegrant.co.uk

Hardie Grant Books (Australia)
Ground Floor, Building 1
658 Church Street
Melbourne, VIC 3121
www.hardiegrant.com.au

British Library Cataloguing-in-Publication Data. A catalogue record
for this book is available from the British Library.

978-178488-000-2

Publisher: Kate Pollard
Senior Editor: Kajal Mistry
Cover and Internal Design: Mina Bach
Cover and Internal Illustrations © Leo Greenfield
Author Picture Photographer, p 156 © Jonty Davies
Colour Reproduction by p2d

Printed and bound in China by 1010

10 9 8 7 6 5 4 3

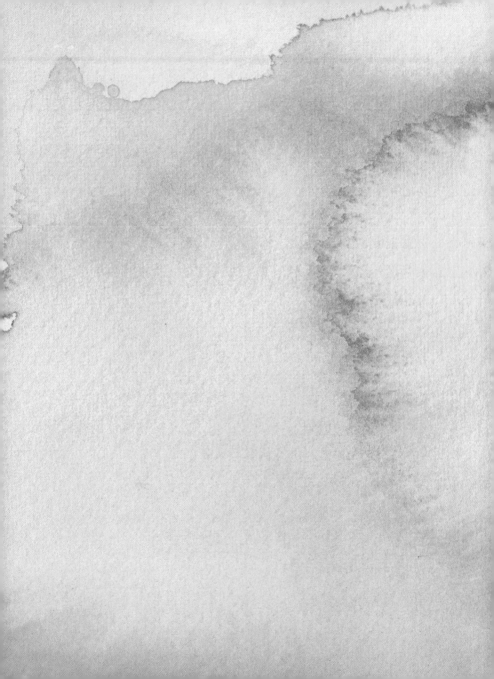